SUPER TRADER

MAKE CONSISTENT PROFITS IN GOOD AND BAD MARKETS

Van K. Tharp, Ph.D.

WITH ILLUSTRATIONS BY JILLIAN COMPHEL

New York   Chicago   San Francisco   Lisbon
London   Madrid   Mexico City   Milan   New Delhi
San Juan   Seoul   Singapore   Sydney   Toronto

This book is dedicated to three very special people in my life.
My wife, Kalavathi Tharp, provides a very special spark in
my life. Without that spark and her tremendous love, this
book would not be possible. My son, Robert Tharp, is one of
the real joys in my life. He's a trader, and he's worked very
hard to understand these concepts. I'm very proud of him.
And my niece, Nanthini Arumugam, has in my mind become
the daughter that I always wished I would have. I am very
blessed to have all of you in my life.

1 2 3 4 5 6 7 8 9 0   DOC/DOC   0 1 0 9

ISBN   978-0-07-163251-5
MHID   0-07-163251-4

This publication is designed to provide accurate and authoritative
information in regard to the subject matter covered. It is sold with the
understanding that the publisher is not engaged in rendering legal,
accounting, or other professional service. If legal advice or other expert
assistance is required, the services of a competent professional person
should be sought.
—*From a Declaration of Principles Jointly Adopted by a Committee of the
American Bar Association and a Committee of Publishers and Associations*

McGraw-Hill books are available at special quantity discounts to use
as premiums and sales promotions, or for use in corporate training
programs. To contact a representative, please visit the Contact Us pages
at www.mhprofessional.com.

This book is printed on acid-free paper.

Contents

iv Contents

Acknowledgments

So many people contributed to the content of this book, and although I cannot recognize each of you individually, to all of you, let me just say thank you. Some of you may have just asked a question that stimulated me to think in a certain way. Some of you may have made a suggestion that started me in a new direction. However, certain people deserve a special acknowledgment because their contribution was enormous.

In particular, I'd like to thank Jillian Comphel for her wonderful illustrations for the book. Jillian is a member of my staff, and I was delighted to find that she was so talented.

I'd like to thank Becky McKay for her work in proofing and editing, and for being an all-round jack-of-all-trades for this book. Thanks, Becky.

I'd also like to thank Cathy Hasty and Melita Hunt for everything they do for me because what they do makes it possible for me to write a book like this. Thanks to both of you. Melita, who used to be the CEO of my company, passed away in early 2009. She was a joy and she will be greatly missed.

Thank you all for your incredible contributions, as well as all of you who contributed in a small way that I've not mentioned directly.

Van K. Tharp, Ph.D.

Preface: The Fate of the "Average" Investor

Countless times people call me up asking for help; however, their plea usually comes with the condition "I don't want to spend a lot of time or do a lot of work because I'm just an average investor." Is that you? Well, Joe Smith considered himself an average investor.

Joe retired in 2003. He had done well during his working years and had a retirement income of $6,500 per month, including Social Security. He had saved about $623,000 as a nest egg for emergencies in his retirement. He still owed about $350,000 on his house. Joe and his wife debated a lot about whether they should pay off the mortgage with their cash. The house payment was nearly $2,000 per month, and if they paid it off, they'd have plenty of money to spend each month and little to worry about.

Joe had lost about 30 percent of his retirement nest egg during the market crash from 2000 to 2003. However, in 2003 the market was going up. Joe figured the worst was over and he probably could make 10 percent per year on his money. That would give them an additional $5,000 per month for spending, which more than covered his mortgage payment. Joe had an advanced degree in civil engineering, and as far as he was concerned, investing wasn't rocket science. He'd do well in the market because he was a smart guy. Chances are, he thought, he could be better than average and get his account back up to a million dollars (the way it was before the 2000 crash).

Joe made a mistake that many people make. He'd spent nearly eight years learning his profession and much of his life staying on top of it. He thought he was smart enough to outperform the market professionals and make 10 percent or more each year as an investor in his retirement. After all, it just amounted to picking the right stocks, and he could do that.

Joe was now 68 years old. His total education in the market consisted of reading three or four books on how to pick the right stocks plus a book about Warren Buffett written by someone other than Warren Buffett. He also watched the financial news regularly, and so he was sure he could make his fortune. He also read several financial newspapers each day, and so he felt informed.

For a while, Joe was right. He made about $120,000 with his investment from 2003 through 2005, and he and his wife spent about half of that. Thus, Joe's account at the beginning of 2008 was worth about $683,000. However, Joe was not ready for the second leg of the secular bear market. On September 30, 2008, the stock market was down over 40 percent for the year, and Joe's account was down 29 percent—it was now worth about $484,000. If he paid off his house now, it would take most of his assets. When the bailout bill passed, he watched the market fall by hundred-point increments each day. Joe was really worried as his account balance approached $400,000.

The CNBC gurus Suze Orman and Jim Cramer said stocks would soon be a bargain: "Don't sell unless you need the money." Didn't they realize that by the standard of just investing and holding, he was down nearly 60 percent from his equity high in 2000? In fact, Joe now needed to make 70 percent on his money just to break even on the year, and he was struggling to make 10 percent per year.

What's the bottom line here? Joe spent eight years getting his education to become a good engineer, yet he treats the investing process as if anyone could do it. It's similar to building a bridge without any training. You can't work like that in the real world, but it's easy to do in the market. In the real world, it could mean a collapsed bridge; when you do it in the market, it means the death of your account.

What does it take to trade successfully, especially in this market? Chances are that we're in a long-term bear market that could last another 10 years. The United States as a country is bankrupt, and no one seems to realize it because we spend money like crazy.[1] Seven hundred billion to bail out troubled debt is just a drop in the bucket. It could get much, much worse.

---

[1] research.stlouisfed.org/publications/review/06/07/Kotlikoff.pdf.

What happens when the baby boomers really need cash for retirement and there is a net flow out of the stock market? There will be a giant sucking sound coming out of the market! Are you prepared for that?

Ask yourself the following questions:

1. Do I treat my trading/investing like a business? Have I prepared for it the way I would for a business?
2. Do I have a business plan—a working document to guide my trading business?
3. Do I make mistakes regularly (a mistake means not following my rules)?
4. Am I following a regular procedure to prevent mistakes?
5. Do I have a tested system?
6. Do I know how that system will perform in different kinds of markets?
7. Do I know what kind of market we are in now and know what to expect from my system in such a market?
8. If I don't, have I gotten out?
9. Do I have exit points preplanned for every position I currently have in the market?
10. Have I developed specific objectives for my trading?
11. Do I understand that I achieve my objectives through a position sizing algorithm? Have I developed a specific position sizing algorithm to meet my objectives?
12. Do I understand the importance of the points above?
13. Do I understand that I create my own investment results through my thinking and beliefs?
14. Do I accept responsibility for that creation?
15. Do I regularly work on myself to make sure that I follow the points above?

Circle all the responses that are true for you. If you haven't circled at least 10 of the 15, you are not taking your trading seriously. Your financial health is in danger.

Here is what you need to do: Don't accept the notion that you are just an average investor and there is nothing you can do. You create your own results, and your results right now come from playing a game with no training.

If you trade for yourself, you need to follow the guidelines in this book. If you do not trade for yourself but have professionals trading for you, do you realize that most of them must be 95 percent invested even in a falling market? They get paid 1 to 2 percent of the value of the assets they have under management. They get paid even if you lose money.

What about your open positions in the market right now? Do you have a bailout point for those trades? That is, do you know what a 1R loss is for you, where R is your initial risk? Or have you already hit a 3R loss (a loss three times bigger than you'd planned) and are starting to ignore the market, hoping that if you don't see it, the fall will stop? Whose fault is it that you are ignoring the market?

When the market clearly has turned down, you should get out. The stock market was signaling a turn in 2007. Figure P-1 shows the trend of the market and at what point the market no longer was going up. This chart shows weekly figures for the S&P 500 since 2003. The 10- and 40-week moving averages are essentially equivalent to the 200- and 50-day moving averages that most professionals use. Note that the 10-week average crossed below the 40-week average in late 2007; that was a clear signal that the market had changed. That occurred at about 1484 on the S&P 500 on March 3, 2009. As of this writing, the S&P 500 bottomed at about 670 in March 2009— nearly a 60 percent drop from its high.

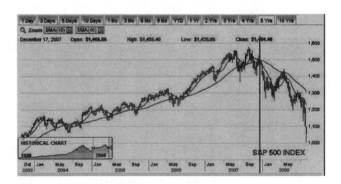

FIGURE P-1 The S&P 500 through mid-2008

There were other signs then as well:

- A head and shoulders top formed, although that was not obvious until about 1400 on the S&P 500.

- If you had drawn a long-term trend line (since 2003), you could have gotten out at about 1400 as well.

- There was an even steeper trendline, which started in 2006, that was broken around 1450.

- My market type analysis has been indicating that the U.S. stock market was basically in a bear mode since January 2008 and that the bull market ended and switched to a volatile sideways market in June 2007.

That's plenty of evidence. If you had a plan to get you out of mutual funds when any of those signals occurred, you would be in good shape. But if you are an average investor, you probably haven't put much time into studying the market. You just think you know what you are doing. What would happen if you tried to build something and put only that amount of study into it?

There is a well-known saying about how to make money in the market: Buy what's going up, and when it stops going up, sell it. Unfortunately, most people listen to the opinions of others and cannot see for themselves what is happening. From April 28, 2003, through January 2008, my market classification model did not have a single week that was classified as bearish: The market was either bullish or sideways. Those were the times to be in mutual funds, as you can see in Figure P-1.

Furthermore, when the bear raised its head in January 2008, you did not want to be in mutual funds or any sort of long-term investing situation involving the stock market. Look at Figure P-1 and you can see that there were no significant bullish periods—unless you were day trading minor up corrections. You just have to look at the chart.

If you are a little more sophisticated, you can buy stocks that are going up and short stocks that are going down. Figure P-2 shows one stock, MYGN, that was going up throughout much of the bearish year 2008. From March through July, there was plenty of evidence that it was bucking the trend, and in July and August it was very strong.

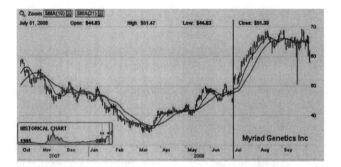

FIGURE P-2 MYGN

However, short candidates have been even better. Most of the darlings of the stock market before the disaster started to hit in July 2007 have plummeted. They include oil stocks, mining stocks, gold stocks, and even tech stocks such as Apple. All of them were good short candidates a long time ago, and most of them were not on the prohibited list of 799 that one could not short. The government for a short time period had a list of prohibited financial stocks that one could not short. This list was valid from September 19, 2008 to October 8, 2008.

By the way, the first part of learning to be a good trader/ investor is to work on yourself. I've told many people these things over the years, but only the ones who clear away the trash in their minds (i.e., nonuseful beliefs and emotions that get in the way) are capable of seeing what's going up and selling when it stops going up.

How about you? Are you going to continue to be an average investor and suffer the fate of other average investors? Are you going to say, "No, this is not for me," and leave it up to professionals who will keep you invested even when the market is going down because they get paid as long as you keep your money with them? Or are you going to take the steps necessary to treat the handling of your money like a business?

For those of you who want to treat investing seriously, perhaps it's time you got an education. This book is divided into five parts, corresponding to the steps I ask people to go through in the Super Trader program at the Van Tharp Institute. The Introduction will give you an overview, and the rest of the book will give you many ideas and methods to help you achieve consistent profits in all types of markets.

Introduction

The Five Steps to Consistent Profits

The goal of this book is to help people develop a full-time trading business that produces consistent, above-average profits under various market conditions. This means that you can perform profitably in up markets (both quiet and volatile), down markets (both quiet and volatile), and sideways markets (both quiet and volatile). To help traders reach this goal, I've designed a five-step approach. If you are reading this, you probably would like that sort of performance. My objective here is to familiarize you with the five steps you must take.

1. Work on yourself and your personal issues so that they don't get in the way of your trading. This step must be accomplished first; otherwise, those issues will interfere with each of the other steps.

2. Develop a business plan as a working document to guide your trading. This plan is not to raise money, which is the purpose of many business plans. Instead, it's designed to be a continual work in progress to guide you throughout your trading career. The business plan actually helps you with all four of the other steps. It also includes an overview of the big picture influencing the markets you will be trading and a method for keeping on top of those factors so that you will know when you are wrong. My view of the big picture is updated in the first issue each month of my free weekly e-mail newsletter, *Tharp's Thoughts*.

3. Develop several strategies that fit your view of the big picture and understand how each of them will perform in various market types. The ultimate goal of this step is to develop something that will work well in every possible market condition. It's not that hard to develop a good strategy for any particular market condition (including quiet and sideways). What's difficult is to develop one strategy that works well in all market conditions, which is what most people attempt to do.

4. Thoroughly understand your objectives and develop a position sizing™ strategy to meet them. Probably fewer than 10% of all traders and investors understand how important position sizing is to trading performance, and even fewer understand that it is through position sizing

that you meet your objectives. Thus, the fourth step is to develop position sizing strategies for each system that will help you meet your objectives.

5. Monitor yourself constantly and minimize the number of mistakes you make. I define a mistake as not following your rules. Thus, for many people who have no written rules, everything they do is a mistake. However, if you have followed the first four steps, you will have rules to guide your trading and can define a mistake as not following those rules. Repeating the same mistake is self-sabotage. By monitoring your mistakes and continuing to work on yourself, you can minimize their impact. People who do this, in my opinion, tend to produce consistent, above-average profits.

Part 1: Working on Yourself

Everything you do is shaped by your beliefs—in fact, your reality basically is shaped by your beliefs. What's a belief? Every sentence I've written (including this one) reflects my beliefs. Every sentence that comes out of your mouth reflects your beliefs, and your beliefs shape your reality. Even who you think you are is shaped by your beliefs.

Let me give you an illustration of how this works. My niece from Malaysia came to live with us when she was 19 years old (my wife and I were putting her through college in the United States). After she'd been with us for a year, one day she said to me, "Uncle, in my next lifetime, I would like to be born beautiful and talented." My niece is very artistic (she sailed through an art course) and sings like she was born to sing. Coming from a liberal arts background, she got a degree in biomedical engineering, graduating cum laude. I think she passes the talent criterion with flying colors. As far as beauty, I'd describe her as one of the most stunningly beautiful women I've ever seen, and everyone who meets her comments on how beautiful she is. Thus, here was an incredibly beautiful and talented woman who because of her beliefs didn't think she had those qualities at all. *Your reality is shaped by your beliefs.* By the way, I've been working on those beliefs of hers since she's been living here, and she's finally coming around.

AUTHOR'S NIECE

Similarly, who you are is shaped by your beliefs about yourself. In addition, you do not trade the markets. Instead, you trade your beliefs about the market. One of the key aspects of working on yourself is to examine your beliefs to determine whether they are useful. If they are not useful, find beliefs that are. This is a key aspect to working on yourself.

You probably will never be free of limiting beliefs or all aspects of self-sabotage during your lifetime, but I consider this step complete when you transform about five very limiting aspects of your life and feel very differently about each one. Once you've accomplished five such transformations, I consider you capable of generally overcoming the future roadblocks that may come up in your trading.

Part 2: Developing a Working Business Plan

The business plan part of trading includes step 1. In fact, a good business plan includes a thorough examination of the person who is doing the trading: beliefs, issues, strengths, weaknesses, goals. Everything you can think of about yourself should be included in this document.

However, the plan also should include many other important things:

■ Your assessment of the big picture and how you'll keep up with it. For example, I wrote about the possibility of a huge secular bear market in 2001 when I first started working on my book *Safe Strategies for Financial Freedom*.[1] I decided that the big picture should include (1) a general assessment of the stock market in the United States and worldwide, (2) a general assessment of the strongest and weakest areas of the world for investments, (3) a general assessment of the strength of the dollar (or your home currency if you are not using the U.S. dollar), and (4) a general assessment of inflation or deflation potential in the future. I also developed ways to measure each of these elements, and my way of keeping up with them is to write a market update on the first Wednesday of each month in my newsletter.

■ Business systems: how you will do research, monitor your data, market yourself (to your family or clients), monitor yourself, manage your cash flow, and keep track of your trades and performance. Basically, running a trading business involves many systems other than trading systems. To have a successful trading business, you'll have to master those other systems.

■ Several strategies that fit the big picture and that work when conditions change. For example, strategies that work in volatile bear markets (e.g., 2008) are quite different from strategies that work in quiet bull markets (e.g., 2003).

■ A worst-case contingency plan so that you'll be prepared for anything major that could upset your trading business. This sort of planning often takes as long as six months to complete.

---

[1]Van K.Tharp, D. R. Barton, and S. Sjuggerud, *Safe Strategies for Financial Freedom*. New York: McGraw-Hill, 2004.

Part 3: Develop Trading Strategies That Work in Various Conditions

In 1999, everyone in America seemed to be a stock market expert. For example, we were giving a stock market workshop at a hotel in Cary, North Carolina, and one of the Happy Hour bartenders said to the other, "Perhaps we should take Dr. Tharp's workshop." The second one responded, "No, I don't need that. I could teach a workshop like that." Similarly, a waiter in a high-class steak restaurant informed us that he was really a trader but worked at a restaurant part-time at night. He'd already made over $400,000 trading and considered himself an expert trader. However, my guess is that those people didn't survive the period 2000–2002, much less the market in 2008. Why? They are different markets, and a strategy of buying and holding high-tech stocks that worked in 1999 has had mixed to horrible results in the years since then.

However, a strategy of buying inverse index funds as soon as the market signaled a clear bear market in 2007 worked wonders in 2008. You need to know what kind of market we are in. I believe that there are six different market types: up, down, and sideways, under volatile and quiet conditions.

Market type might be different for you, depending on your investment trading perspective. However, I look at 13-week rolling windows. When I look at many such windows and take the absolute value of the 13-week change, I find that the average change (going back to 1950) is about 5.53%. Thus, if the absolute value change of a 13-week window is less than that amount, I consider it a sideways market. If the absolute value is greater than 5.53%, I consider it bullish if the market is up and bearish if the market is down.

I then measure volatility by the average true range (ATR) as a percentage of the close. The 13-week ATR as a percentage of the close over the same period averages to 2.87%. Thus, when that number is above 2.87, I consider the market volatile, and when it is below it, I consider it quiet. Table 1-1 summarizes 58 years' worth of data according to market type.

Typically, most people attempt to develop one strategy that works in all kinds of markets. The waiters and bartenders, and most others for that matter, usually fail. However, there is good news. It's not that hard to develop a strategy that will work well

	Bear	Sideways	Bull	
Volatile	10.08%	20.31%	10.96%	41.35%
Quiet	1.83%	37.98%	18.84%	58.65%
	11.91%	58.29%	29.80%	100.00%

TABLE 1-1 Fifty-Eight Years of Market Data

in each kind of market. What's difficult is to find one that will work well in all conditions. However, you don't have to do that if you simply monitor market conditions.

Part 4: Learn How to Meet Your Objectives

In our workshops we typically play a marble game. Marbles are placed in a bag to represent a trading system. For example, 20% of a trading system may be 10R winners. Since R is short for what you risk, a 10R winner is one for which you make 10 times what you risk. The system also may include 70% 1R losers, meaning that when one of those marbles is drawn, you lose whatever you risk. Finally, the system may include 10% 5R losers, meaning that when those marbles are drawn, you lose five times what you risk. The marbles are replaced after they are drawn so that your odds remain the same after each draw.

Now, some of you might be thinking, "But you'll lose 80% of the time. How can you possibly make money?" Let's say there are 100 marbles in the bag. If you total the R values of all the marbles in the bag, you'll find that they add up to +80R. That means that on the average you'll make 0.8R per pull over many, many marble draws. Thus, the expectancy of the system is 0.8R (after 100 trades, you'll probably be up about 80R). If you risked about 1% on each marble pull, after 100 pulls you'd probably be up more than 80%. Perhaps now the system doesn't seem so bad.

When I play the game, I usually provide the audience with different incentives. For example, I might say that if you go bankrupt, you are out of the game and have to pay a fine of $10. I also might say that if you end the game down 50%, you have to pay a fine of $5. I also could say that if you lose money by the end of the game, it will cost you $2.

On the positive side, I might say that if you make money, you'll win $2. If you make 50%, you'll win $5. I also might say that if you make the most money, you'll win whatever is left in the pot, say, $100.

Note how my incentives set up a number of objectives for the game. For example, here are three possible objectives:

1. To win the game at all costs, including risking bankruptcy. The person who wins the game usually has this objective.

2. To win at least $2 and make sure you don't lose more than $2. Note that this is an entirely different objective.

3. To win the game but make sure you don't go bankrupt. Again, this is an entirely different objective from the first two.

When I tell people how to strategize about the game, I suggest that they answer the following questions:

■ Who are you?

■ What are your objectives?

■ What is your position sizing strategy (i.e., how much) to reach your objectives?

■ Under what conditions might you be willing to change your position sizing strategy?

If 100 people play the game (starting with $100,000) and all get the same trades (i.e., the same marble pulls randomly done and replaced), chances are that there will be 100 different equities at the end of the game. You also will be able to group people according to their objectives. For example, those who are trying to make money and have minimal losses will have a small fluctuation of equity of about 5% to 10%. However, those trying to win the game will have huge equity fluctuations that range from bankruptcy to making millions.

My point here is that the game illustrates what is really important to trading success: the "how much" variable of position sizing. Thus, a key step for anyone wanting consistent profits is to develop a strategy with a positive expectancy and then develop a position sizing strategy that maximizes the probability of meeting one's objectives. This hugely important step is largely ignored by most traders and investors, including most professionals.

Part 5: Taking Steps to Minimize Your Mistakes

What happens when you don't follow your rules? You make a trade when your system didn't tell you to trade. You are supposed to get out when your stop is hit, but you don't get out. Your position sizing is way too big on one particular trade. Those are all mistakes, and mistakes can be very costly.

We've done some preliminary research on the cost of mistakes, and the results suggest that for leveraged traders, mistakes can run as high as 4R per mistake. If a person makes 10 mistakes in a year, that person could find his or her profits dropping by about 40R. That means that if he or she made 50% on the year, that investor could have made nearly 100%. If he or she lost 20%, then mistake-free trading could have made that person profitable.

For long-term investors with wide stops, mistakes probably cost about 0.4R per mistake. The total cost per year with 10 mistakes is about 4R. However, the average investor is lucky to make 20% per year, and so 10 mistakes could easily cost an investor 20% of his or her profits.

The final step that you must concentrate on is to minimize the impact of mistakes on your trading. This amounts to developing a disciplined routine in your trading and continuing to take step 1—working on yourself.

PART 1

Working on Yourself: The Critical Component That Makes It All Work

The Components of Trading Well

I'm a neuro-linguistic programming (NLP) modeler and a coach for traders. As an NLP modeler, I encounter a number of people who excel in something, determine what they do in common, and then determine what beliefs, mental strategies, and mental states are required to perform each task. Once I have this information, I can teach those tasks to others and expect to get similar results. My job as a coach is to find talented people and make sure they learn and follow the fundamentals.

I remember doing a workshop with the Market Wizards Ed Seykota and Tom Basso around 1990. All three of us agreed that trading consists of three parts: personal psychology, money management (which I subsequently renamed position sizing in my book *Trade Your Way to Financial Freedom*[1]), and system development. We also agreed that trading psychology contributes about 60% to success and position sizing contributes another 30%, which leaves about 10% for system development. Furthermore, most traders ignore the first two areas and don't really have a trading system. That's why 90% of them fail.

THE COMPONENTS OF TRADING WELL

---

[1]Van. K. Tharp, *Trade Your Way to Financial Freedom,* 2nd ed.. New York: McGraw-Hill, 2007.

Over the years I've done extensive modeling in all three areas, and I now disagree slightly with our conclusions in 1990. First, I would argue that trading psychology accounts for 100% of success. Why? This conclusion is based on two findings. First, people generally are programmed to do everything the wrong way. They have internal biases that seem to lead them to do the exact opposite of what is required for success. For example, if you are the most important factor in your trading, you should spend the most time working on yourself, but the majority of people totally ignore the "you" factor in their success. Read over the checklists in this part that deal with good trading. If you've worked extensively in all the areas listed, you are probably very successful and are certainly a rarity.

Second, every task I model requires that I find the beliefs, mental states, and mental strategies that are involved. All three ingredients are purely psychological, and so it's hard not to conclude that everything is psychological.

I now think that there are five components to trading well:

1. **The trading process.** The things you need to do on a day-to-day basis to be a good trader.

2. **The wealth process.** Exploring your relationship with money and why you do or do not have enough to trade with. For example, most people believe that they win the money game by having the most toys and that they can have it all right now if their monthly payments are low enough. This means that they save zero dollars and are over their heads in debt. If this is you, it also means that you don't have enough money to trade.

3. **Developing and maintaining a business plan to guide your trading.** Trading is as much a business as is any other area. The entry requirements are much easier because all you have to do is deposit money in an account, sign a few forms, and start trading. However, the entry requirements for successful trading require that you master all the areas listed here. That requires a lot of commitment, which most people do not have. Instead, they want trading to be easy, fast, and very profitable.

4. Developing a system. People often consider their
system to be the magic secret for picking the right
stocks or commodities. In reality, entry into the market
is one of the least important aspects of good trading.
The keys to a moneymaking system are elements such
as determining your objectives and the way you exit
a position.

5. Position sizing to meet your objectives. We've
discovered through our simulation games that 100 people
at the end of a set of 50 trades will have 100 different
equities. (They all get the same 100 trade results). This
extreme variability of performance can be attributed to
only two factors: how much they risked on each trade
(i.e., position sizing) and the personal psychology that
determined their position sizing decision.

Based on the five components of trading well, rate yourself
by asking the following questions:

■ **How well have I mastered the discipline of trading
well each day?** Do I do a daily self-analysis or a daily
mental rehearsal to begin each day? If not, why not? I
will give you a lot of ideas about how to improve in
this area in the remainder of this book.

■ **Do I really have enough money for trading to make
sense?** If you do not, you probably need to work on
yourself and the wealth process.

■ **Do I have a working business plan to guide my
trading?** If you don't, you are not alone. We estimate
that only about 5% of traders have a written business
plan. Then again, perhaps you've heard that only about
5% to 10% of all traders are really successful. The next
part of this book will guide you toward developing this
kind of working document.

■ **Do I have a set of objectives thoroughly written out
to guide my trading?** Most people don't. How can
you develop a system to meet your objectives without
having objectives?

■ How much attention have I paid to the "how much" factor, position sizing? Do I have a plan for position sizing my system to meet my objectives? It is through position sizing that you either meet or fail to meet your objectives.

■ How much time do I spend working on myself? You have to overcome your psychological issues and develop the discipline necessary to carry out the processes described above, which are necessary for success.

Most of the items described here could be the topic for an entire book. However, my intention was to give you an overview of what is required for successful trading, and my job as a coach is to find talented people and coach them on following the fundamentals I've described them here.

Do an Honest Self-Appraisal

A peak performance trader is totally committed to being the best and doing whatever it takes to be the best. He or she feels totally responsible for whatever happens and thus can learn from mistakes. These people typically have a working business plan for trading because they treat trading as a business; that business plan gives them the confidence to do what they need to do to make large returns from the market and learn from the mistakes they make.

The first section of this book is not about some hot new investment. It's about how to be in the best possible condition mentally to trade at a peak level. My favorite cartoon character is SAM, the trading tiger, shown here looking inside himself. SAM will be guiding us through the process of successful trading/investing.

LOOK INSIDE YOURSELF

Getting Started: Some Concepts You Must Master as a Trader

First, you need a strong initial evaluation of yourself and what you need to do to improve your performance. Look at it this way. Suppose you are in the middle of the desert. There are no roads, but you have a map indicating where you are to go. However, what's missing is an indication of where you are now. Remember that you are in the middle of the desert. How can you get where you want to go when you don't know where you are? Similarly, how can you work on yourself as a trader if you don't know much about yourself? That's the situation most people face. They think they know themselves well, but they really don't know anything about themselves. Have you, for example, made an inventory of your beliefs about yourself? Are you those beliefs?

Second, if you want something, you must practice "being" it. Being, in other words, comes before doing or having. In my opinion, most people want to trade well, but their primary concern is how to do it and have success. You must practice being a successful trader first. From that state of mind you will get information about what to do, and that will produce what you want to have. Many people also believe that they must struggle and work hard to get ahead. This is the antithesis of the statement above about "being" successful. If you believe you must struggle to become successful, you probably will struggle a lot.

Third, many traders have what I call the perfectionism-complexity complex. In other words, what you have is never quite good enough. It can always be improved in some way. There is always another exit or another entry that will make it better. What this means is that you always will be struggling with new ideas. Consequently, you never will get to the real issue of trading and just being a trader, doing trading. Instead, there is always one more thing to test—always one more thing to do—and never enough time to just relax and trade. Give up complexity and move toward simplicity.

The best traders are always those who practice simplicity. For example, at a recent seminar one trader remarked, "I just buy what's going up. If it goes against me, I get out immediately. If it goes in my favor, I let it run. I've made a lot of money doing that." That is simplicity, but you can do it only if your mind and spirit are pure and you are paying attention to what the market is doing. It's purity of spirit that makes the difference. This particular trader always asks for internal guidance before beginning the trading day. I tend to believe that makes a big difference.

Fourth, many traders—and people in general—have low self-esteem. If you don't believe you are worthwhile, that belief will tend to dominate everything else. You may believe, "If I can just make money trading, I'll feel better about myself." However, that belief actually is composed of two beliefs: low self-esteem and the belief that low self-esteem will be "fixed" by trading success. Unfortunately, that doesn't seem to be the case. Low self-esteem always seems to dominate and produce behaviors to justify itself unless, of course, you are aware of it and do the kind of self-work that will improve your self-esteem. If you think that life is a struggle, it's probably because of your low self-esteem.

The key to all these issues is to understand yourself and realize that you are the root cause of your results in trading. When you do that, you have started on the road to success.

Think about the last loss you had in your trading. What caused it? Who was responsible for it? If your response is anything other than yourself (e.g., the market, my broker, bad advice), you are not taking responsibility for your results. You will repeat mistakes over and over until you understand this. In contrast, if you are willing to accept total responsibility for your investment results, you begin to understand all the mistakes you've made and are able to correct them. The market will become your financial university. Moreover, you will realize that you are the most important factor in your trading or investment success. If you understand that, you are way ahead of the crowd.

I once had a call from a gentleman in England who had been working through my peak performance home study material. He said, "I've been working through your course for over six months. It's helped me realize a lot about myself, but there is one thing it hasn't done. It hasn't given me a positive expectancy system." The ironic thing about that statement is that I had not attempted to provide a methodology in that course; it is about how to become a peak performance trader/investor.

If you want to be good at something, you must design a method that fits you. That is possible only if you design the methodology to fit your beliefs, meet your objectives, and match who you are.

Psychology is far more important than methodology. In fact, psychology is part of methodology. For example, when we attempt to help people develop a reasonable method that works, they resist it strongly because they have so many biases that keep them focused on the wrong aspect of trading—areas that have nothing to do with success. It is very difficult to show them the correct direction.

The best thing you can do to increase your income from the market is to determine how you are blocking yourself. This should be done at two levels. Whenever you develop a trading business plan, a large part of that plan should have to do with introspection. Take a look at all your beliefs. Are they useful beliefs, or do they hinder you in some way? What are your strengths and weaknesses? What about yourself can't you see clearly because you are part of it? You should consider doing this sort of assessment at least once each quarter.

The second self-appraisal you need to make is at the beginning of the day and perhaps even hourly throughout the day. What's going on in your life? Are you ready to face the markets? How are you feeling? Is some sort of self-sabotage surfacing in you? For example, are you starting to get too confident? Are you starting to get too greedy? Do you in any way want to override your system? The best traders and investors constantly do this sort of self-assessment. If you want to make more money in the market, perhaps you should start doing it too.

To help you with your self-assessment, I developed a quick 17-point questionnaire you can use to evaluate yourself. Take it and pass it on to your friends; I'm sure you'll all get some insights into your performance. Answer each question with true or false.

1. I have a written business plan to guide my trading/ investing. _____

2. I understand the big picture about what the market is doing and what is affecting it. _____

3. I am totally responsible for my trading results, and as a result I can correct my mistakes continually. (If either part is false, all of this statement is false.) _____

4. I honestly can say that I do a good job of letting my profits run and cutting my losses short. _____

5. I have three trading strategies that I can use that fit the big picture. _____

6. For trading strategy 1 I have collected an R-multiple distribution of at least 50 trades (i.e., from historical data or live trading). If you don't know what an R-multiple distribution is, which you'll learn later in this book, you haven't collected one, so answer "False." _____

7. For trading strategy 2 I have collected an R-multiple distribution of at least 50 trades (i.e., from historical data or live trading). _____

8. For trading strategy 3 I have collected an R-multiple distribution of at least 50 trades (i.e., from historical data or live trading). _____

9. For each of my trading strategies, I know the expectancy and the standard deviation of the distribution. _____

10. For each of my strategies, I know the types of markets in which they work and in which they don't work. _____

11. I trade my strategies only when the current market type is one in which the strategies will work. _____

12. I have clear objectives for my trading. I know what I can tolerate in terms of drawdowns, and I know what I want to achieve this year. _____

13. Based on my objectives, I have a clear position sizing strategy to meet those objectives. _____

14. I totally understand that I am the most important factor in my trading, and I do more work on myself than on any other aspect of my trading/investing. _____

15. I totally understand my psychological issues and work on them regularly. _____

16. I do the top tasks of trading on a regular basis. _____

17. I consider myself very disciplined as a trader/ investor. _____

Give yourself one point for each true answer. Be honest with yourself.

Fill in your score here_____

Let's take a look at how you rate.

- **14 or more.** You have the makings of a great trader/ investor and probably do well in the markets.

- **10–13.** You have a lot of potential but probably are making some major mistakes; for many of you, these may be psychological mistakes.

- **7–9.** You are way above average but haven't graduated to the big leagues yet. You are like a high school football star trying to move to the NFL.

- **4–6.** You are better than the average investor on the street but have a long way to go to hone your skills. You probably need to work on yourself, your discipline, and your trading strategies.

- **3 or less.** You represent the average trader/investor. You probably want someone to tell you exactly what to do and expect to make big profits now; when it doesn't happen, you look for a better advisor or guru to help you. Guess what? It doesn't work that way. If you answered "True" to questions 3 and 12, you have some potential and, if you are willing to commit yourself to excellence, could move to the top of the scale in a few years.

You'll get a strong boost toward improving your score from going over the material in this book, but you must do the necessary work.

What's Your Trading Type?

Can everyone become a good trader? I tend to think not. Take, for example, the Turtles experiment in which 1,000 people responded to ads in the *Wall Street Journal, New York Times,* and *Chicago Tribune* to be trained by Richard Dennis and Bill Eckhardt in the Turtles system. The respondents all had to take a 52-item questionnaire. The top 40 were flown to Chicago for an interview, and fewer than half of them were selected and trained to become Turtles. Although Richard Dennis won the bet, Curtis Faith[2] says that he thought the experiment was a draw. Some of the traders were good, but many were not that great, and that was after an extensive selection and training process!

THE STRATEGIC TRADER   THE DETAILED TRADER   THE INDEPENDENT TRADER

WHAT TRADER TYPE ARE YOU?

As an NLP devotee, I've always believed that if someone can do something well, that skill can be taught to anyone else. I have modeled all aspects of the trading process and developed workshops to train people in how to become great traders. However, not everyone has the mentality and commitment to do the work it takes to follow through on the training.

Because of my findings over the years, I've come to the conclusion that there are certain trading types. Some types are natural traders, whereas others need to go through a real struggle to master what's important to trading.

We developed what we call the Tharp Trader Test, in which we divide the universe of people into 15 different trader types.

---

[2]Curtis Faith, *Way of the Turtle.* New York: McGraw-Hill, 2007.

For each type, I've found a prototype for that trader and developed a set of strengths and challenges for each one. Find out what trader type you are by going to www.tharptradertest.com. Spend a few minutes answering a questionnaire, and you'll find out your type and what you need to do to be successful. Do it now. It takes only about five minutes. Write your trader type in the space here: _____.

About half the trader types have a high potential to become successful, with the strategic trader being the most natural and the fun-loving trader being the least natural. It was interesting putting the scale together because one of my jobs was to find a prototype trader to fit each category. It was pretty easy to find good models for the trader types that tend naturally to be successful. Paul Tudor Jones is a good example of a strategic trader.

However, the trader types that were not a natural fit had very few examples for me to pick from because those kinds of people simply don't make good traders. For the fun-loving trader, I ended up choosing the CEO of Starbucks. He's definitely a fun-loving type, and because he's invested in his own company, I can call him a successful investor/trader. However, he is certainly not a Paul Tudor Jones and never could be.

Now that you've figured out your trader type, here are the 15 types, with some challenges specific to each one:

1. Strategic trader. This type of trader has a great chance of success but is (a) likely not to recognize emotional mistakes, (b) lean toward perfectionism, and (c) have a strong desire to be right.

2. Planning trader. Again, this type of trader has an excellent chance of success. Your major challenge is the desire for excitement and the need to be right. You easily could become bored with trading and do things to lessen the boredom and thus limit your profits.

3. Detailed trader. The detailed trader has a good chance of success, but you could be so into the details of what you are doing that you miss the big picture.

4. Administrative trader. You may be overly critical of yourself but not recognize mistakes that are right in front of your eyes. Furthermore, under stress you may question your commitment to trading because you don't find it satisfying. An administrative trader also has a good chance of success.

5. Facilitative trader. This kind of trader has an above-average chance of success. However, you could have a problem with logic and ideas because you are always finding something new. Furthermore, you may need external confirmation of your ideas, beliefs, and systems.

6. Innovative trader. You have an above-average chance of success. However, you probably want external confirmation for everything you do and have a strong need for a mentor. Furthermore, you may tend to abandon a good system prematurely if it goes against you because of your emotional reactions.

7. Values-driven trader. You have an above-average chance of success in trading but find that you must do things your way. In addition, discipline, follow-through, and attention to detail will always be a problem for you. You also may find trading boring and do things to fulfill your need for excitement.

8. Independent trader. You are driven by logic and could easily reject systems that work well because you don't understand them logically. Furthermore, your trading could dominate your time and leave you socially isolated. That said, you have a good chance of success if you apply yourself.

The remaining seven types have a much more difficult time becoming successful in the trading arena.

9. Socially responsible trader

10. Spontaneous trader

11. Supporting trader

12. Accurate trader

13. Artistic trader

14. Fun-loving trader

15. Adventurous trader

If you are in one of these categories, it's not an impossible task, but you will have to work harder and make a stronger commitment.

Commitment

My job as a coach is to find talented people and make sure they learn and follow the fundamentals. But what is a talented trader? What do I look for in people before I coach them?

One of the first things I look for is commitment. Most people come into trading having accumulated a lot of money in another profession. We see a lot of doctors, lawyers, engineers, information technology (IT) professionals, and the like. All those professions require a lot of training to master the skills involved. You cannot walk into a hospital with no training and say, "I'd like to do some brain surgery today." Instead, it requires 16 years of basic education, 4 years of medical school, serving as an intern, and then completing a residency period. It requires a lot of dedication and commitment to begin to practice as a doctor.

Let's look at trading. What is the entry price for trading? Perhaps you watch a show on television in which some guru tells you what stocks he or she likes. You then open up a brokerage account by filling out some paperwork and deposit some money. You then can buy some stocks and wait for your profits. Entry into trading is that easy! It's designed that way so that other people can take your money in fees and commissions. People who trade that way have the same results that an off-the-street brain surgeon might have: The patient dies. In this case, the death is to your account.

Earlier, I covered some of the elements of successful trading:

1. Doing what's required on a daily basis and going through the trading process
2. Having a strong enough money mindset to have sufficient funds to trade with
3. Having a business plan to guide your trading
4. Having a good system or perhaps two or three good systems
5. Having proper position sizing in place

Behind all of those elements is the key to everything: your personal psychology.

Working extensively in these five areas requires immense commitment, the same commitment that is required to become a brain surgeon. That makes sense: Great traders make a lot of money, but a person has to be willing to do what it takes to be successful.

This requires that you have a goal in mind and an intense desire to reach that goal so that you'll do whatever it takes to get there. This is the essence of commitment. However, most people don't realize what is necessary for trading success because it's not required for entry into trading. Although I can teach people what's important, I cannot give them the commitment to do it, and potential traders must have an intense commitment to get through the elements of successful trading.

Imagine someone who is driving around but has nowhere in particular to go. We'll call him Henry. Henry stops at a fast-food restaurant and orders a sandwich. The sandwich turns out to be the worst one he's ever had. It's been burned and dropped, and the sauce on it is spoiled. As a result, Henry complains and then talks to the other restaurant patrons about the food. The manager is not very happy and kicks Henry out. Now Henry is infuriated

**IF YOU AREN'T COMMITTED, YOU TEND TO DO
A DANCE WITH ANY OBSTACLE YOU ENCOUNTER**

and starts a campaign through the local newspaper to have the restaurant closed. This goes on for weeks, but Henry is willing to spend the time because he doesn't have anything else to do.

When people are not committed, they run into distractions. Henry had no place to go, no motivating force behind him, and so he just attached himself to a bad-tasting sandwich and his campaign against the restaurant took up a lot of his time. When you are going from point A to point B and are not committed to reaching point B, you tend to do a dance with any obstacle you run into instead of just moving around it.

> When you are going from point A to point B and you are not committed to reaching point B, you tend to do a dance with any obstacle you run into instead of just moving around it.

Now imagine someone who has an important appointment that she must make within the next three hours. She still has a 2.5-hour drive to make the appointment. However, she stops at the same restaurant and gets the same bad sandwich. Does the sandwich suddenly consume her? No, she may complain and throw it away, but then she moves on because she is committed to something else. She either stops at another restaurant to buy something to go or skips lunch. To a committed person, the most important thing is the destination.

When you are committed to becoming a good trader, you do whatever it takes and little things don't throw you off track. When distractions arise, you go around them and focus on your goal. That's the power of commitment, and commitment is essential to trading success.

In my experience, people who are not committed find numerous distractions that take up most of their time. They complain that they are too busy to do what it takes to be successful as a trader, but most of their time is preoccupied with distractions.

A football coach looks for talented players who have the commitment to follow the fundamentals and do what it takes to be the best. You may be the most talented athlete ever, but if you don't have the commitment to be the best, the coach probably will drop you from the team. I find myself doing exactly the same thing with traders: I look for talented people with a lot of commitment because they are the ones who will be successful.

What is your commitment to trading excellence? Read over the elements of successful trading that were given. How committed are you to achieving them? This is the real entry requirement for trading success.

To illustrate my point, here are a couple of letters that I've gotten and my responses to them.

> *Dear Dr. Van Tharp:*
> *What's a reasonable goal for me as a trader? Can I make a living trading? Can I make millions trading? Is that reasonable for a former professional?*
>
> *I'm aged 46, and I'd like to move into full-time trading. I've accumulated about $200,000 in cash. What is possible for me given my age and goal to become a full-time trader?*
> *Sincerely,*
> *E.R.*

> Dear E.R.,
> Your trading goal is up to you. You can certainly become a full-time trader. That is probably possible within a year to 18 months. You can certainly take a million dollars out of the market, and you could reach the stage where you take a million dollars out of the market each year. It depends on what you are willing to do.
>
> However, there are a number of questions that you will need to ask yourself because each scenario has a different answer.
>
> How much do you love trading? How committed are you to being a full-time trader making millions? Are you willing to work 12 to 16 hours a day, six days per week, for the next five years? Are you willing to use at least four to six of those hours a day to start your own trading business? Are you willing to spend another hour or two a day developing probably the most valuable skill you could ever have, self-knowledge?
>
> Are you willing to give up most of your free time—at least until your trading business is off

and running soundly? And are you willing to think about trading when your family is still enjoying the things that you used to do together? Will you do whatever it takes to be the best (including discipline and full responsibility for your results)? You would need to start by spending at least the first six months really working on yourself, looking at all your psychological patterns and developing ways to overcome any personal obstacles.

In addition, you will need another four to six months to develop a business plan that will be the basis of your trading business. Most people don't treat trading like a business. And most businesses fail because people don't plan.

Are you willing to learn a new way of thinking about the markets? This means thinking in terms of a reward-to-risk ratio, understanding that risk is what you lose when you lose in a trade, and understanding that position sizing is the core of how you'll work to meet your profit targets. Most of what you have learned about the markets needs to be turned upside down, examined, and then thrown out as garbage. Could you handle it?

Would you be able to develop at least three systems that fit the big picture? And are you willing to work on these systems enough that they become great systems?

I mention all this because all these things are required if you are serious about being a top trader who earns a lot of money in this field. I have made the studying of top traders my vocation and have written books on all these subjects for years.

It's all up to you. Are you willing to do the necessary work or is the goal too lofty?

> *Dear Dr. Van Tharp:*
> *I'm just an average investor. Tell me how to make*
> *a lot of money, but make it easy and not*
> *complicated. I don't have the time, and I'm an*
> *average investor.*
> *Thanks, R.M.*

Dear R.M.,

What you don't seem to understand is that trading is a profession. If you are a doctor, you spent years of study learning to practice your profession well. You can't just walk in off the street and perform brain surgery even if you've read a textbook about it.

Similarly, if you are an engineer, you also spent years learning your profession. You can't just start building a bridge without the training behind it. The bridge probably would fall apart.

So when you tell me you are an average investor, you are telling me that you have no training and that you don't plan to spend the time getting the training. That means you'll probably get average results, and average investors generally lose money.

Do What You Love

I have a pretty good taste in art, I think. I can go into most art galleries and find the painting I like best, and it is usually one of the most expensive pieces in the gallery. I can do that for all types of art except abstract art, which I don't understand.

With that introduction, I'd like to mention that I've watched my wife study art and go from a beginning artist to a fantastic artist in a period of about 5 to 10 years. Many of her pieces might now be the type of work that I'd gravitate to in a gallery. Here are a couple of examples. The first one is an abstract piece that she painted for our office. I don't usually like abstract art, but I love this piece, and we have it mounted so that you see it as soon as you enter our office.

"PASSION": A KALA THARP ABSTRACT

The second one is a piece that she modeled after a French artist whose work we both admired. I personally think it is as good as the work of the French artist whose style she copied.

My point is not to tell you how good she has become but to tell you what she did to get that good. I think her movement from amateur to master occurred as a result of two things she did. First, she went to an Avatar workshop in Ireland. She didn't think that she got that much from the workshop, but her painting took a leap forward afterward. She said that somehow it freed her creativity. She wasn't worried about the results. Instead, she just started to express herself.

"GARDEN BY THE LAKE": A KALA THARP ACRYLIC[3]

The second thing she did was to start a self-improvement program in a book called *The Artist's Way*[4] by Julia Cameron. As she worked through the program, I noticed that her art was getting better and better. At this point, what I noticed was that she really loved her work.

So what does this have to do with trading and success? People who are successful in a range of fields start some sort of program of self-improvement. They move into what they love to do, and as they commit to it (because they love it), all sorts of things happen to make it work for them.

One day, as she was going through her program, my wife announced to me, "No one has more self-sabotage than me." I was delighted to hear her say that because when people begin to think like that, I know they've come a long way in their self-work program. In fact, just her saying it told me that she was way ahead of most people, who are so numb to their self-sabotage that they are not even aware of it.

Most of my Super Traders spend at least six months or even a year doing psychological work. When they realize how much self-sabotage they have and decide to move through it, I know they'll make it. I don't expect people to clear out all their major issues involving self-sabotage, but once they've transformed on at least five major issues (and know that they are different as a result), I feel confident that they can move around any other obstacles that come into their pathway.

---

[3]Visit kalatharp.com to see more of Kala's art.
[4]Julia Cameron, *The Artist's Way,* 10th anniversary ed. New York: Tarcher, 2002.

Personal Responsibility

It's time to talk about the most important trait that any trader can have: personal responsibility. Why is personal responsibility so important? One of my beliefs is that YOU are the most important factor in your trading. It's not your system because YOU both produce and execute your system. It's not position sizing because YOU must execute the proper position sizing algorithm to produce results to meet YOUR objectives. And it's not the market, because you don't really trade the market, YOU trade YOUR BELIEFS about the market.

You produce the results you get as a trader. When you understand that, you realize that you must make changes if you want more effective results. YOU must produce the changes.

At some of my workshops I play the simulated trading game we discussed earlier. In that game everyone gets the same trades, and the only real decision is how much to bet (thus, it's really a game about position sizing). In fact, since everyone gets the same trades, the only two factors operating in the game are position sizing (deciding how much) and personal psychology. However, in a game with a positive expectancy, with 100 people playing with the objective to win the game, I'll typically see a third of the room go bankrupt, another third of the room lose money, and the remaining third make very nice profits.

Typically, I ask the people in the audience to pull out marbles to represent the trades that a system might produce randomly. In addition, I ask the same person to keep pulling trades (i.e., marbles) until he or she gets a winner. That means that if there is a long losing streak (and there usually is), it will be associated with the person who pulled the marbles out of the bag for that streak. I then ask the audience, while pointing to the person who pulled out the losing streak, "How many of you think you went bankrupt because of Bill?" Amazingly, quite a few of the bankrupt people raise their hands. The problem with that assumption is that nearly every simulated trading game will have a long losing streak (it's designed that way), and that streak always will be associated with the person who pulled it. Thus, if you believe that person was responsible, you'll probably make the same mistake over and over. You'll go bankrupt in many games, and it will always be "Bill's" fault.

Furthermore, there are many possible responses to the question "Why did you lose money in the game?"

- It was the fault of the guy who pulled all the losing marbles (trades).
- This is a stupid game, and it doesn't reflect real trading.
- It's random chance and has nothing to do with me.
- I didn't have a good system.
- I'm a stupid idiot.

All those responses are excuses, and they won't help you improve. There is only one response that will help you improve: "I risked too much money on a number of the trades. My position sizing strategy was inadequate. That's why I lost money or went bankrupt."

When you understand that, you can fix the problem. When you give any of the other excuses, you just compound the problem and will repeat those mistakes.

Now are you beginning to understand why taking personal responsibility for your trading is so important?

When you look at your trading results and say, "I created that result," you are in charge of the process. If you don't like the result, you can start to look for the mistakes you made. When you find the key mistakes that actually produced your results, you can make changes and get better results. That is why personal responsibility is so important and why I look for it in all of my Super Traders.

Do you like the results you produced as a trader in the last 12 months? If not, what mistakes did you make and how can you correct them? Ask yourself the following:

- Do I have a business plan to guide my trading?
- Do I have a worst-case contingency plan?
- Do I have several positive expectancy systems that are well tested for this market climate that I can trade?

■ Do I have something else that will work if the market type changes?

■ Do I even pay attention to the type of market we are having?

■ Do I regularly work on myself as the core of my trading results?

If you answered no to any of those questions, you have some real clues about why you got results you didn't like in the past. These, by the way, are only a few of the questions you could ask yourself.

What Are Your Excuses?

By now you should have many ideas about how to improve your trading. There is probably no good reason not to spend a month (or six months) developing a good plan to work on yourself and implementing many of these ideas. What is stopping you?

Take some time and write down your excuses. Do some of those excuses and justifications look like the following?

- I just didn't have the time.
- If I do it, I'll probably miss something and just lose more money.
- This material isn't for me. When I bought it, I was looking for something simple. I didn't think there would be so much work involved.
- Dr. Tharp really doesn't understand me. If he did, this material would be easier.
- My life is going fine. I don't have any problems, and I just don't need to deal with all this stuff.
- Working on myself is scary.

WORKING ON MYSELF IS SCARY

■ I have too many distractions and cannot focus.

■ I'm right, and Dr. Tharp just doesn't get it.

■ I need to really study this stuff, and I just can't seem to find the time.

■ It would be much easier if my spouse understood this and how important it is.

When you make excuses of this nature, you do it simply so that you can be right. You are basically saying that you like certain beliefs because they are right. It doesn't make you happy. It doesn't make you successful. However, you do get to be right, and if that is what's important to you, then so be it.

WHAT ARE YOUR EXCUSES?

There is a better strategy with which to evaluate a belief: Ask yourself, "Is it useful? Is it getting me what I want? Is it working?" One of the basic presuppositions of NLP is that if something doesn't work, do something else. Almost anything else will produce different results.

If your trading isn't working, change what you are doing. If your trading system isn't working, change how you approach the system (your exits and your position sizing). If your life isn't working, change the way you approach your life. Ask yourself—whatever it is you are facing—"Is it working or is it not working?"

Life is a process. There is no success or failure, only feedback. You've been getting feedback about what you've been doing for a long time. Are you willing to change now? It's never too late. You're never too old. Today is always the first day of the rest of your life, so begin now.

Imagine that you are responsible for everything that has happened to you up to now in your life. Didn't we just discuss that topic? When you finally decide you are responsible for your own life—for what has happened in the past—you will find that you get an immense rush of freedom. You can decide right now what you want, and you are in charge of making it happen.

Empower Yourself

It's possible for traders to tap into one of three general attitudes when they approach the market. The first attitude is one of pessimism, the second is one of randomness and/or neutrality, and the third is one of empowerment. The first attitude never works, the second attitude seldom brings much success, but the third attitude, when properly done, guarantees success.

EMPOWER YOURSELF

Let's imagine that you have the immense power to create the results you want from your trading activity. A good reason to make this assumption is that you do have such power. We've been talking about it. Now, if you had such power, what do you think would happen if you approached your trading from a viewpoint of pessimism? You would lose money. No matter how good your system was, you'd figure out a way to lose money.

If you approach the market with neutrality—and you have this power to create your life—the best you can do is perform at an average level. You certainly won't add any personal energy to the market, and I suspect that your performance will be substandard.

Let's look at the third option: approaching trading with an attitude of empowerment. In my modeling work with traders, I've observed that all good traders know they will win at the end of the year. I might take that one step further and say that great traders know they probably will win at the end of the month (or week). What does that imply? It implies a great deal of *faith*. You must believe in yourself and in your trading. You must know deep in your heart that you have won and feel grateful for your success.

Faith is like a magic power that propels you to greatness. For example, let's take a look at a few Bible quotes:

> *Let it be to you according to your faith.*
> Matthew 9:29

> *If there is faith in you even as a grain of mustard seed, you will say to this mountain move away from here, and it will move away; and nothing would prevail over you.* Matthew 17:20

> *If you can believe, everything is possible to him who believes.* Mark 9:23

> *Whoever should say to this mountain, be moved and fall into the sea, and does not doubt in his heart, but believes that what he says will be done, it will be done to him.* Mark 11:23

> *Therefore, I say to you, anything you pray for and ask, believe that you will receive it, and it will be done for you.* Mark 11:24

Incidentally, I used to avoid using a lot of spiritual references because I found that many people's beliefs about spirituality were both very strong (the essence of who they were) and very narrow (if you went beyond their boundaries, you entered dangerous territory). However, my objective is to help people change, and I've found that the most powerful change is at the spiritual level. Thus, it is time to begin to open up the spiritual basis of trading.

When you have faith, you take personal responsibility (even if it amounts to God acting through you) to another level. When you operate at that level, you are definitely a peak performer.

Write Down Your Beliefs

Earlier, I talked about doing an honest self-appraisal. What does that mean? Let's go deeper into yourself and the way you create your trading results.

Let's look at couple of the simple steps that are involved in peak performance trading. I've developed a procedure to help traders reach peak performance called the Trader Reinvention Paradigm. Part of this paradigm involves setting a goal for yourself that stretches you and puts you outside your comfort zone and then helps you make a commitment to achieving it. Getting to it involves regularly focusing on your progress toward the goal and asking, "How did I produce that result?" and "How can I do something different and move closer to my committed goal?"

When you do this, it will tend to stretch you, and you will have to think continually about how you produced that result. This tip is designed to help you assess that answer.

You do not trade the markets—no one does. That may sound surprising to many of you, but what you really trade are your beliefs about the market. Furthermore, your ability to do that is tempered by your beliefs about yourself.

I'd like you to do an exercise. Write down your beliefs about yourself. Those beliefs typically start in the following ways:

- I am . . .
- I feel . . .
- I experience myself as . . .

If this sort of exercise is new to you, when you first do it, you'll probably write down a bunch of your positive attributes. Furthermore, you'll probably have trouble writing down more than 20 or 30 of those beliefs, but you actually have hundreds.

Let's say you think for about five minutes and come up with the following items:

- I am a fairly good trader.
- I feel positive about my potential.
- I like myself.
- I am fairly astute in thinking about the markets.

■ I am intelligent.

■ I am creative.

You know there are a lot more, but after 15 to 20 minutes of thought that's all you can come up with. Okay, that's a start, but now I'd like you to continue the exercise each time you make a trade, either opening a position or closing it.

Let's say it's Monday morning and you open two positions in the market. After doing so you continue to assess yourself and notice your thoughts:

■ I feel really excited.

■ I like fast-moving stocks.

Okay, you've gained some insight into yourself.

By midafternoon, the market is in a steep decline and three of your stocks are down $500 on the day. Notice your thoughts:

■ I feel angry about that position. I just got in, and it's going against me.

■ I'm not going to let them take advantage of me this time. I'll hang on until it goes back up.

You've just gathered some more insights about yourself. Keep this up until you've written down 100 or more statements that reflect you and your feelings. When you do that, you'll have a lot more insight into the way you produce your trading results and will be starting on your way to becoming a peak performance trader.

Now that you've written down 100 beliefs, examine those beliefs by asking yourself six questions about each one. I call this the *Belief Examination Paradigm*.

1. Who gave me this belief? My parents? My peers? The media? School? Or did I select it for myself?

2. What does this belief get me into? (Write down at least five things.)

3. What does this belief get me out of? (Again, write down at least five things.)

4. How does this belief limit me?

5. Is this a belief I want to keep because it is useful or is it a belief I want to get rid of because it limits me? (By the way, at a very deep level all beliefs limit you in some way, but some are still useful for the level at which you now find yourself and are thus worth keeping.)

6. If the belief is not useful, can I simply drop it for something more useful, or is there a charge (emotion) holding it in place?

If you find that there is a charge holding your belief in place, you need to release the charge to free the belief. We'll discuss how to do that later.

Let's look at one example of a belief: *Good performance comes from picking the right stock.* Let's put that belief through the Belief Examination Paradigm.

■ **Who gave me this belief?**
I hear this all the time. There are lots of books about how to pick stocks. I watch experts give their picks on the financial channel. Everyone talks about how important it is, and so it must be true.

■ **What does this belief get me into?**
I spend a lot of time looking for the right stock.
I listen to people who think they are good stock pickers.
I read books about stock picking.
Once I've picked the right stock, that's all I have to do—just buy it and hold on to it.
I question my stock picking criteria to see if I can improve them.

■ **What does this belief get me out of?**
I don't spend time analyzing myself, and so it gets me out of personal responsibility.
It gets me out of looking for my own mistakes if the stock failed. Instead, I simply assume that I did a poor job of stock picking.
I avoid other important aspects of trading such as exits and position sizing.
I don't do much planning because that has nothing to do with stock picking.
And I certainly don't pay attention to the market generally because the right stocks should be good all the time.

Can you begin to see how some of the aspects of this belief might not be that useful? I hope so. Let's move on to the next question.

■ **How does this belief limit me?**
The limitation here is obvious. It makes me think that entry and stock selection are the most important aspects of making money. If I don't do well, I think that something is wrong with my selection criteria. Instead, I should be able to focus on myself. I should focus on the other parts of the system and whether the system is working. In addition, I need to know how the system will be able to perform in various market types and how to position size to meet my objectives. This belief causes me to ignore those things. (Of course, most people would not be able to give this answer because the belief would limit their knowledge of the other factors.)

■ **Is this belief useful?**
Since stock selection is one of the least important aspects of trading, this belief is probably not that useful.

■ **Can I change it, or does it have a charge on it?**
I should be able to change it, but there is a little fear about dropping it because I'm not convinced about the other things.

This person probably needs to release the fear.

Imagine the control you'll have over your life after you've completed this exercise on 100 beliefs. What would happen if you applied it to 1,000 beliefs? Whether you do that will depend on how useful you believe the exercise to be—which just proves the power of your beliefs—and how committed you are to being in control of your life and your trading account.

Enjoy Your Obstacles

Let's look at some of the processes you can use to work on yourself. There are many of them in later parts of this book; find the ones that seem useful to you and begin the process.

You already know that a committed person with a clear goal will encounter an obstacle, refocus on the goal, and move out again toward the goal. An uncommitted person, in contrast, may do a dance with the obstacle that could last a long time. In fact, most people spend their entire lives doing dances with obstacles that get in their way.

In any endeavor in life, you have up and down periods. Dealing with the market has many such periods. To profit from the up periods, you have to tolerate or even enjoy the down periods; to enjoy the profits, you have to get through the losses. Perhaps it would be useful if you could celebrate your losses.

CELEBRATE YOUR LOSSES

I'm an NLP modeler. As mentioned earlier, that means that if someone does something well, I can figure out the essence of what that person is doing by understanding his or her thinking.

Thus, when such a person goes from point A to point B easily and effortlessly, I can determine how he or she does it and teach that skill to other people. Some people make money through trading easily and effortlessly, and I've been studying those people for 25 years.

It turns out that one of the major problems people have in going from their current location to their desired goal is all the walls or obstacles they run into each day. There is a common solution to these obstacles: Make them okay. If you enjoy bumping into the walls, it is usually easy to refocus on the goal.

If you're in the market, one of biggest obstacles you'll face is the wall of losses. It's fairly difficult dealing with the markets if you are not willing to lose. It's actually almost impossible. It's like walking but wanting to use only your left foot, avoiding your right foot. That doesn't work, and neither does trading without losses.

When you want to be right, you're not dealing with the obstacles. Instead, you're forcing things. When you want to make a profit out of today's trade even though it's a big loser, you're not dealing with today's obstacle. Enjoy the obstacle— embrace it—and be willing to accept it. If the market tells you it's time to get out at a loss, do that.

Good traders typically have some point in the markets at which they know they must get out of a position to preserve their capital. Taking this loss is essential. It preserves your capital, and so you should enjoy doing it.

However, if you don't understand that the loss has nothing to do with being right or wrong—it's just part of the process— you could turn it into a monster. What then happens is that you fight with each loss, and in the struggle the losses typically get bigger. For example, if you are afraid of a $500 loss and won't take it, you easily could watch it become a $1,000 loss. The $1,000 loss, when not taken, can easily become a $2,000 loss. The net result is a losing trading system.

Think about it. If you have this problem with losses, you easily could turn a good trading system into a losing system. If you don't realize that it's your problem with losses, it might become the trading system's problem. Or if you are following someone's advice, it might become your advisor's problem or your money manager's problem.

Guess what? Quite often traders take the relationship they are having with the market and transmute it by developing a different system or trading with a professional money manager. Now the old problem they used to have with the market of not accepting what the market gives them becomes a similar struggle they are having with their system or with the new advisor. Instead of giving up on the market after a string of losses just in time to miss the really big move, they avoid their system until it is doing really well. When it is showing tremendous profits, they jump on board, only to be blown away by the market, and the same thing happens when they invest with money managers. This desire to be right motivates them to jump to the top money manager when she's hot, only to go through a big string of losses.

Psychologically, if you don't come to grips with your obstacles and embrace them, you will find another way to repeat them. Realize that the walls occur because they are there for you to bump into. When you accept this fact and embrace it, you'll accept bumping into walls. Strangely enough, you then hardly even notice that the walls are there. The result will be a new level of success in the market.

Good traders realize that they can have 10 to 20 losses in a row. It's part of the business of trading. It happens, so just accept it and move on. If you have trouble accepting it, you need to realize that the problem is you and deal with that.

Trade through "Mindfulness"

What would happen if you could just pay attention to what the market is doing right now? You'd be totally in the present with no preconceived ideas or biases to influence you. If you did that, your trading probably would accelerate to a new level. You can trade that way if you practice mindfulness.

For example, in October 2008 a friend of mine had lost a lot of money in the markets. I told him to get out. I said that we were in a major bear market and he should just get out until it ended. He followed my advice.

The next week the Federal Reserve lowered the discount rate. The market moved up on the news, and he called me, wanting to get back in the market. I said that when the market starts going up again, it will be obvious. Short-term reactions to news tend to be large in bear markets; however, if you just watch what is going on, it is obvious. Most people have trouble with this. They can't watch what is going on because their heads are so full of chatter. The solution is to trade through mindfulness.

Mindfulness first came to my attention as a form of meditation in which you simply quiet your mind and then "watch your thoughts" as they come up. When a thought pops into your mind, you notice that it is there and then release it. That's all there is to the meditation, but it can have a profound impact on your life if you do it regularly.

Mindfulness is also a state of being. The Harvard psychologist Ellen Langer has popularized the term through two books: *Mindfulness* and *The Power of Mindful Learning*.[5] She defines mindfulness as a state of being in which one is likely to be (1) creating new categories, (2) welcoming new information, (3) looking at things from multiple perspectives, (4) controlling the context, and (5) putting the process before the outcome.

Creating New Categories

Mindfulness is the opposite of mindlessness. Mindlessness means living by your conditioning. It means assuming that all

---

[5]Ellen J. Langer, *Mindfulness*. Reading, MA: Addison Wesley, 1989. Ellen J. Langer, *The Power of Mindful Learning*. Reading, MA: Addison-Wesley, 1997.

your beliefs are fixed and true so that all you can do is find evidence to support that truth. Mindfulness, in contrast, is the continual creation of new concepts and categories with no real attachment to their truth.

For example, think about your last day of trading. What was it like? You might say, "I put on some long trades and some short ones. I also closed out some trades—some at a profit and some at a loss. In between, I watched the market."

Even if I offered you money for everything you could list that you did yesterday with respect to trading, you still probably couldn't come up with much more than what I just listed. Yet you did so much more. You probably experienced a thousand different emotions, which you've forgotten. You probably read 100 news items. You probably talked on the phone to some people. But unless I mention those things to you, you probably wouldn't think of them.

Most strong opinions rest on global categorization:

- The market went up yesterday.
- We're in a C wave of an ABC correction.
- I lost money yesterday, but I followed my system.
- We're in an up move in a secular bear market.
- I should pay attention to what is going on now in the market.

All those statements reflect global categories that you probably use to form your opinions. What would happen if you formed new categories of thought about the market? Think about the market in great detail. Who are the different players? What do you think each of them is doing with respect to the market? Call people you know and notice their reactions and their perspectives. Break old thinking patterns by creating new categories and you'll step up your trading.

Welcoming New Information

New information continually impinges on all living creatures, and their ability to survive depends on their openness to that information. Research has shown that people undergo temporary psychological damage if they are deprived of new information for any length of time. If they are deprived of sensory input, young animals become severely impaired later in life. You need sensory information to stimulate you.

WELCOMING NEW INFORMATION

Most people are exposed to new information continually, and so the lack of it is not a problem. However, most of us tend to filter, generalize, distort, or delete most of that information. Becoming more receptive to the information that is coming in to you is a major step toward improving your performance as a trader.

Looking at Things from Multiple Perspectives

There are at least three general positions or perspectives from which information can be viewed. The first perspective is the "I" position: "How does this information affect me?"

The second perspective, position 2, is how it affects another person directly: "What is that person's perspective?" The second position might be that of the person who takes the opposite side of your trade or perhaps the person who is making the market for you. Looking at new information from that person's perspective may be a valuable thing to do.

The third perspective is that of the neutral observer who is watching all the other participants. This is like someone out in space who can see what everyone else is doing and then view it all from a global perspective.

These three perspectives were crucial in Einstein's thinking processes. This was part of how he formed his great ideas about relativity. Those perspectives are also the basis for some of the most powerful change work I know about. Try them on. Of course, there are many possible players for positions 1 and 2. You can try on numerous possibilities and gain tremendous insights as a result. You'll gain choice in terms of how to respond, empathy for other people, and the ability to change your behavior much more easily.

Remember that most people have "good" reasons for behavior that you might consider negative. The intentions behind those behaviors are good. If you close out a trade early, are you "nervous" or are you "cautious"? If you fail to take a trade, is it because you are "afraid" or because you haven't totally developed and tested your plan for trading? Typically, the behaviors you most want to change are the mirror images of the qualities you value most. Thus, if you are having trouble "pulling the trigger," you probably value a thoroughly tested plan and don't have one.

Controlling the Context

Much of your behavior is context-dependent. For example, many professional traders know it is possible to lose $20,000 in a trade, perhaps paying $1,500 in trade costs in the process. However, the same traders are much less likely to pay $1,500 to attend a course that could reshape their trading and help them avoid many of those losses. The thinking behind such logic is that the loss is a cost of doing business whereas the course is an unnecessary cost. Notice what happens to the logic if you switch it around and start to think of the course as being essential to doing business well. It becomes much more significant than the losing trades, especially since it may save the trader many thousands of dollars in a single year. Of course that depends on the course you select.

People who practice mindfulness are aware of the context in which they are interpreting events. They are also willing to shift contexts to determine the impact on their behavior and their thinking. As a result, they give themselves much more choice and are much more likely to make money.

Ask yourself the following questions:

- How am I interpreting my losses?
- What is the context in which I am viewing all my trading?
- How does trading fit into the scheme of things in my life?
- What if I shifted the context on just one of these questions?

Putting the Process before the Outcome

People can imagine themselves taking gradual steps, but great heights seem totally forbidding. Yet when you take enough gradual steps, you'll reach great heights.

If you are concerned with the final result—the outcome— you probably will have problems attaining the outcome. However, if you concentrate on the process of getting to the outcome, you are much more likely to arrive at your destination.

Every outcome is preceded by a process. You will not make money trading unless you follow a predetermined plan and stick to that plan. That's why you should pat yourself on the back every day if you can honestly say that you totally followed your rules throughout the day. Every Super Trader arrives at that stature by taking one trade at a time. The primary difference between that person and the average trader is that the Super Trader probably continued to follow his plan every single day. The Super Trader probably made very few mistakes.

What can you do to practice mindfulness in your trading?

1. Do a 20-minute mindfulness meditation each day for at least a week. If you practice watching your thoughts (and releasing them as soon as you notice them), you can be satisfied that you are doing the exercise appropriately.

2. Keep a regular diary of what is going on in your life. Do it for a few days before you start the mindfulness meditation and then keep it up. When you've completed a week of mindfulness meditation, look at your diary and notice how your life is different.

3. Bring mindfulness into your trading and investing by doing the following:

   a. Imagine yourself taking the other side of every trade that you actually take. What does that position feel like? Also imagine yourself being a neutral observer who watches as you and the other person both take a position in the market. What do you think that person would think?

   b. Look for new information about each new trade. What information are you normally accepting and what information are you normally rejecting?

   c. When you do something you don't like in your trading, notice the context in which you are interpreting not liking it. How else might you interpret that behavior? What other intention might cause that behavior? Perhaps those other intentions are something you value highly.

   d. Concentrate on the process of trading—following your rules. In fact, at the end of each day ask yourself a simple question—"Did I follow my rules?" If you did, pat yourself on the back. If you don't have any rules, you obviously didn't follow them. Think about it.

These exercises are powerful if you do them. If you don't do them, they are meaningless. Are you going to do them? If the answer is no, ask yourself why not. It is probably because you don't believe they will help you. If that's the case, put that belief through the Belief Examination Paradigm I showed you earlier. Perhaps you are not committed to trading success. If that's the case, what are you committed to? What do you love to do?

Make Friends with
Your Inner Interpreter

Think about a problem you have with your trading. It could be almost any problem. Perhaps you have trouble taking profits too soon. You might get angry when a trade gets away from you. Perhaps you frequently second-guess yourself. Whatever your problem is, write it down. You can apply this exercise to almost anything you think might be a problem.

Once you have identified that problem, write down several statements about it. Why do you think you have the problem? What caused it? What's your reaction to the problem? Your statements could be almost anything: "Why do I keep doing that?" "That behavior just shows that I'm stupid." "I just can't seem to control myself." "The problem is really nothing, but it just seems to continually repeat itself."

These statements are your interpretation of the problem. In fact, without this interpretation, you probably wouldn't have a problem. Thus, perhaps it's important to work with your inner interpreter.

MAKE FRIENDS WITH YOUR INNER INTERPRETER

You need to use your imagination with this exercise. Be willing to play like a child.

1. Now that you have listed a problem and some statements about it, ask yourself how you can best explain the way the problem happened. Perhaps you've already done that with one of your statements. If you have not, that's your next statement. Write down what you hear. In addition, notice the qualities of the voice making the statement. Where do you hear the voice; which direction does it come from? Whose voice is it? Is it your own? Is it someone else's?

2. Now find two more problems and repeat step 1. Make sure the problems have some emotional significance for you.

3. Look at the three statements you've written about how your three problems happened. What do they have in common? Notice how permanent and pervasive the statements are. Also notice the overall personality behind the voice.

4. Rewrite the three statements and make them more optimistic and specific to a time or occasion and to the place where they happened. Make them impersonal to separate them from your behavior.

5. Let's assume that a part of you—your inner interpreter—is responsible for these statements. Where does this part of you seem to live? Is it on one side of your head? Is it at the front of your head? Or perhaps it's coming from your heart. Notice once again where the voice seems to come from.

6. Think of this part of you as a friend that you created for a positive reason. Thank this part for helping bring you to where you are today. It's really been a friend to you, and you need to acknowledge it.

7. Once again, now that you are in communication with your inner interpreter, ask it to come up with even more positive reasons for your three experiences.

8. Move your interpreter voice to another part of your body, say, your right shoulder. Change the tone of the voice.

Make it sound like a cartoon character or a famous celebrity you like. Try moving it again and giving it another new voice. Listen to that voice go over your new excuses and perhaps some more optimistic ones.

9. Notice how you feel about your interpreter now.

10. Now let your inner interpreter go where it feels best. That may be its original spot or a new place in your body. Give it the voice you find most reassuring.

If you get stuck in this exercise, it is okay to make up an interpreter. In fact, you really never make up anything. When you make something up, you are just bringing it up from your unconscious mind.

You'll find that when you do this, you suddenly have much more control over your feelings. Your interpretations are never reality. Instead, they are just judgments, feelings, or beliefs about a particular event. They feel real because they give you an emotional response. However, emotions have nothing to do with reality. They are simply coming from you.

The nice thing about such interpretations is that they are changeable. They cost nothing to change but give you tremendous benefits. It's now time to put your inner interpreter on your side. After all, it is your friend.

Here's how one person, let's call him Bill, went through this exercise. When Bill thought of a problem, it was the criticism he got from his spouse whenever they talked about trading. He could hear her voice in his head, saying, "Trading is nothing but gambling. It's a waste of time and has no redeeming value."

Bill wrote down some statements about the problem and came up with the following:

- I married the wrong woman. She's an idiot, and she just doesn't understand what I do.

- Her parents instilled an old work ethic in her, and trading doesn't fit that work ethic; that's why she gets upset.

- She wants security and doesn't feel comfortable when I tell her about trading.

He noticed that the voice was kind of high-pitched and always seemed to come from the right side of his head. It seemed to be coming from an elevated position down into his head. When he repeated the exercise with several more problems, the voice had the same qualities and came from the same place.

When he tried to move the voice, he first put it in his throat and made it raspy. That didn't feel comfortable at all. However, he didn't have any problem moving it between his eyes and giving it a child's voice. That seemed very comfortable.

When he made new, more optimistic interpretations of situations, he found that it was quite easy when he kept the voice in the new position. As a result, he decided to give his inner interpreter a new home. Now this part seems to appreciate him much more and gives him very few problems.

Try this interpreter exercise at least once a week for the next four weeks. Notice what happens after you do it and keep practicing. You could be adding a very valuable tool to your life.

These exercises are useful only if you do them. Decide how important they are to you and then do them.

Learn to "Dissociate"

If you think about peak performance trading, you could look at a market genius and how that person approaches her craft. However, you also could look at a genius in some other area and notice if some of his behavior could be applied to trading. In that regard, I've been thinking about how Einstein would think about the modern markets. I learned that one of the things Einstein did well was to dissociate. He used imagery to step out of his body and assume another perspective.

Try this exercise for yourself. During each part of the imaginary adventure that follows, notice what your thoughts are and what your experience is like.

Here is the first imaginary scene. See yourself (your whole body) on a movie screen skydiving. See yourself in the airplane with the parachute attached. Now see yourself getting ready to jump. After you jump, see yourself free-falling for about 10 seconds and then pull the rip cord. Notice what happens when you pull the rip cord; it's like the parachute pulls you up in the air. Now watch yourself gently floating down to the ground. That's called being dissociated.

Repeat the same scenario, only now see it out of your own eyes. Notice your hands and feet as you are sitting in the plane getting ready to jump. Now move over to the door, get yourself ready, and then jump. Notice yourself moving rapidly away from the plane as you free-fall. After about 10 seconds, see your hand as you pull the rip cord and notice what the experience of your parachute opening is like. Now feel yourself floating gently down to the ground. That is called being associated.

Note that the scene was the same for both experiences— you were jumping out of an airplane. Yet the images, both of which were imagined, were quite different.

We live most of our lives in an associated state. As a result, everything seems real. Our feelings seem real. Our beliefs seem like reality. Yet that is the case simply because we seem to be part of it. What we are thinking seems to be all there is.

As soon as you assume another position—dissociated— your experience changes dramatically. Your thoughts are different. Your experiences are different. Yet is this second experience any more or less real? Neither one: It's just another experience.

This quality of assuming other perspectives, especially this dissociated perspective, is common to many great people in many fields. Einstein is just one example. Great quarterbacks have claimed to have the perspective of being above the entire football field (even while they are playing) so that they can see the entire field in a detached manner.

Imagine the perspective that would bring for anyone who could do it.

Michael Jordan has claimed to be able to imagine floating over the basketball court and from that perspective seeing everything that is going on. Perhaps that explains why he seems to know where everyone is. Again, think of the advantage such a skill would give you.

I did two interviews with the former fund manager Tom Basso. Jack Schwager, who gave him the nickname Mr. Serenity, interviewed him in *The New Market Wizards*.[6] In my interview with Tom, he revealed that his ability to dissociate was one of the secrets of his success. Here's a little of what he said:

> In situations where I felt I needed improvement or in which I wanted to improve my interactions with other people, I would just play key events back in my head—figuring out how others handled the situation. . . . I've always thought of it as some Tom Basso up in the corner of the room watching Tom Basso here talking to you in this room. The funny thing about this secondary observer was that as time went on, I found the observer showing up a lot more. It wasn't just at the end of the day anymore. As I got into stressful situations, as I started trading, doing more interacting with a lot of people, getting our business off the ground, dealing with clients, etc., I found that this observer was there to help me through it. If I felt awkward or uneasy, then I was able to watch myself do it. Now, I have this observer there all the time.—Excerpt, *Course Update* #9, December 1990.

---

[6]Jack Schwager, *The New Market Wizards*. New York: New York Institute of Finance, 1989.

A fundamental presupposition of NLP is that if one person can do something, everyone else can do it too. Since being able to move to another perceptual position is one of the critical aspects of genius and greatness, it's important to start practicing it.

Here's an exercise. At the end of the day, replay the day in your mind, especially critical junctures in the day. Do it from a disassociated point of view in that you watch yourself going through the day. Once you've completed the exercise, write down what you notice about yourself.

How can you apply this to your trading? Here is a simple exercise for when you feel that you are not trading well. Simply stand up and walk away. Move to a different part of the room and observe yourself. Notice what you looked like sitting there in the state you were in. What did you do with your body? How did you hold yourself? What did your face look like? What was your breathing like?

After you've observed all those things, notice how you feel now. You are no longer in that body. Instead, you are watching yourself from a dissociated perspective. All the feelings and emotions should be gone. If they are not, make sure you are watching yourself.

Now ask yourself some questions: What resources do I need to be able to handle this situation like a Super Trader? Do I need confidence? Do I need the courage to get out? Do I need some perspective? How would I look if I had those resources?

Imagine yourself in the same situation with those new resources. See yourself sitting there full of those resources and notice how different the situation is when you bring those resources to the table.

Chances are that things are quite different. Now we'll find out the real application of this exercise. Go back to the situation and become what you were just imagining. What is that like? Chances are that it's an entirely different perspective on the situation, and chances are that you are performing at a totally different level.

That's the power of dissociation. Practice this technique at least once a day for the next week. The more you do it, the easier it will become.

Achieve Balance in Your Trading/Investing

Achieving balance certainly would rank as one of my top 10 tips to you. First we'll talk about balance between profits and losses. If you can understand that portion of it, it will be easier to understand the importance of balance in other areas.

ACHIEVE BALANCE IN YOUR TRADING

We live in a world of polarities: good-bad, up-down, young-old, happy-sad. The "win versus loss" polarity is just one example among many. In most cases, we tend to judge the polarity in that we prefer one side and dislike the other side. However, one of the secrets to life is to make both sides of the polarity okay. What does that mean?

This is hard for most people to understand, but perhaps it will be easier when I explain it in terms of profits and losses. You cannot be a successful trader if you are not willing to have both profits and losses. Both are a significant part of the trading process.

Most people don't understand this concept. They want to be right all the time. They want to make money on every trade.

Yet that will not happen because losses are a part of the trading/ investing process. When you understand this relationship, you can come to terms with losses and make them okay.

A natural part of the trading process is to have a point at which you must unload a position or trade at a loss to preserve your capital. Those losses happen to most people about half the time or more, and you must make them okay or neutral.

If a loss is not okay, you will not take it now. When you're not willing to take a loss, it usually gets a little bigger. When it rains, it pours. As a result, it becomes even harder to take—much more painful. If you didn't take it the first time, as it becomes bigger, you will be even less likely to take it. What's likely to happen? It probably will become even bigger. The cycle typically continues until the loss becomes so big that you have to take it. This typically occurs when you get a margin call from your broker.

However, investors may never get a margin call if they are not margined. Instead, they tie up valuable capital in a falling investment that may last forever. There are probably millions of investors right now who are hanging on to losing investments that have occurred since 2000 because they are waiting for the market to come back. As you can see, you must make it okay to take losses.

The other half of the equation is also important and is equally puzzling: You can't put too much importance on gains. People who value profits too highly tend to take them quickly. Why? Because if they don't take them, they are afraid the profits will get away from them.

An example of this was pointed out to me in the case of real estate investors. A group of investors got into a real estate deal that started to lose money. Instead of getting out and taking their loss, they elected to stay in and ride it way down. When asked why they didn't get out of a bad investment, their comment was, "We haven't gotten our money back yet."

The same investors subsequently got into another real estate deal. It started to become profitable very quickly. In fact, it rose to 100% profit and more. However, the investors who held on to the bad investment now sold out quickly at a small profit. When they were asked why they sold, the reason was, "We lost money on the other deal, so we wanted to make sure we got our money back on this one."

This concept of balance is very important and applies to any polarity you can think of—not just profits and losses.

Overcoming a Stuck State of Mind

When you are marching toward a goal such as trading excellence, you may do so by overcoming obstacles. When your focus is on problems you have, such as lack of funds or limited resources or limited knowledge, you probably are going to generate feelings of guilt, anger, or frustration in yourself. Little is accomplished with such mental states. You feel stuck, and your orientation toward "stuckness" tends to persist.

ARE YOU STUCK?

Whatever you cannot accomplish in life is a model of a stuck state. Early in life, when you tried to accomplish something, you probably were attacked by some sort of unforgiving failure. The problem was not so much the failure as the intensity of the attack. That event planted a psychological stop sign in front of you whenever you started in certain directions. That psychological stop sign has an impact that is as strong as the original bashing. It creates internal conflict when you attempt to accomplish certain things, with part of you wanting to go on and part of you wanting to retreat. You oscillate back and forth, producing a stuck state of mind.

When people are stuck, you can see the oscillation in their bodies. Typically, they see two pictures. With the first blink, they see what they want, and with the second blink, they see their psychological stop sign. You can observe this in sales professionals, for example. The salesperson wants to make the sale, yet she hates rejection. She decides, "I can do this, but I don't have a worthwhile product" or "My product is good, but people just don't respond to me." The result is usually the stuck state of procrastination.

The same thing goes for a trader. One part of the trader says, "Get out of the trade; it has hit your exit point, and you need to cut your losses." Another part says, "Stay in the trade; it'll turn around, and you don't want to take a loss now." Usually the result is a stuck state.

I've seen hundreds of people in stuck states. One state that was particularly striking involved a man in his forties who still lived with his parents. He wanted to go out on his own, but something held him in place, keeping him dependent on his parents. When I saw him, he had decided that trading was a way he could earn money to escape. However, he'd become stuck because earning enough money to escape would result in an extreme negative state. As a result, he found he could not pull the trigger.

Every time we put something off, some dream or goal, we start to oscillate. We want to achieve the dream or goal, but we also want to avoid the pain that it takes to accomplish the task. The result is "e-motion"—a lack of motion outside ourselves and an intense motion (e-motion) inside ourselves.

Some Simple Solutions

When you are stuck, the more effort you put into trying to unstick yourself, the worse off you become. It's a little like being stuck in quicksand: The more you struggle, the more quickly you sink. The first solution is always to relax and move slightly in the direction that is opposite to what your instincts tell you. For example, a pilot going into a nosedive must push gently into the dive to get air flowing under the wings properly. At that point he can begin to control the airplane. Similarly, when you start to skid in your car, you must steer into the skid until you gain control over the car although your natural reaction is to do the opposite.

If you are stuck in your goal of becoming an excellent trader, try doing the opposite of your instincts. If you must take a trade, make it okay not to take the trade. Instead, move toward working on your emotions.

The second solution is to focus on what you want. When you focus on limitations, you feel the emotions of the stop sign or the limitation. When you focus on what you want to achieve, you begin to see possibilities and new resources that open you up. What is your focus?

The third solution is to focus on *being* what you want to be. If you want to be a great trader, don't focus on what great traders have or do; focus on their state of being. What is it like to be a great trader? What is it like to step into their shoes?

I do an exercise in a workshop in which I ask students to step out of a stuck state to notice what they look like. This dissociates the person and takes her out of the stuck state. I then ask them to imagine a great trader in the same situation. What would that trader look like? What would he be like? I then ask them to step into the beingness of the great trader. The result is almost instant transformation. Try it.

Does Failure Motivate You?

I've been reading a wonderful book by Jerry Stocking titled *Laughing with God*.[7] In that book the following dilemma is brought up, and I'm going to rewrite the conversation a little to make it pertinent to trading/investing.

> **God:** *Do you want to win without losing?*
> **Trader:** Of course.
> **God:** *If you win, you must lose as well. But you weren't honest with me. You said that you'd like to just win. If that were the case, you'd win much more often.*
>
> *The possibility of failure motivates you much more than the possibility of success. Your whole society thrives on failure or at least the fear of losing. If there were not the possibility of losing, you could not take any credit for success. Making money in the markets would seem meaningless for you.*
>
> *Think about it. What if you recorded a sporting event and someone told you the final score? Would you still watch it? Probably not because it's the uncertainty of the outcome that keeps your attention.*
>
> *You could make money on every trade, but that wouldn't be fun. You'd lose the uncertainty you love and yet pretend to eliminate.*

The last statement may get to some of you. But what if it's true? Ed Seykota said in *The New Market Wizards*[8] that people get what they want out of the market: excitement, punishment, and a justification for their emotions. I've certainly seen plenty of evidence to suggest that his observation is true. But the conversation gets even more interesting.

---

[7]Jerry Stocking, *Laughing with God*. Clarkesville, GA: Moose Ear Press, 1998.
[8]Jack Schwager, *The New Market Wizards: Interviews with Top Traders*. New York: New York Institute of Finance, 1989.

> **God:** *You know what will happen in the market*
> *because the future is an illusion you invent.*
> *Ignoring what you know at the soul level proves*
> *how much you love uncertainty. You use the*
> *illusion of the future to keep yourself locked*
> *in time.*

To make this conversation more meaningful, imagine that you are 100% accurate on every trade. You know every top and every bottom on every stock. You are never wrong about a trade. Suppose you just entered the market and made $10 billion in a year. Would you keep going if it were that easy? Would $10 billion be enough? Would you keep trading?

Perhaps your response is, "Sure I would! I'd get all the money in the world." Would that be interesting? I tend to doubt it. Trading is interesting only because of the possibility of losing. You are now in a position where you can buy anything or do anything because you will never lose money on a trade. Would you still trade? Why or why not?

Everything in this section may be made up. Nothing may be true, but I'd like you to assume (act as if) it is true. Just pretend that it's true. When you do so, what happens to you inside? How do you feel about trading? Would you keep on trading? If so, how often? If not, why not? What does that tell you about yourself? Is it the uncertainty that keeps you in the game? Would you keep trading if you had all the money in the world? Why? What do your answers tell you about yourself?

I encourage you to do this exercise and notice what comes up for you. How many trades would you take if you had no uncertainty about the outcome? What do your answers tell you about yourself?

A Note for Your Consideration

There are many books that claim that the text "came from God." I don't know whether such books actually come from God, but if they give me new ideas to ponder, I find them very exciting.

If it stretches your beliefs to think something came from God, assume that someone made it up, but at the same time imagine that it might be true. This one gave me a lot of new ideas, and if you open yourself enough to do the same thing, you might find the ideas quite expansive.

Also notice if there were any buttons pushed by this exercise. If there were, ask yourself, "What's the belief behind my buttons getting pushed?" When you find the belief, go through the Belief Examination Paradigm with it. If you actually do the exercise, you'll find that the belief is limiting you. They key question now is, "What is the charge behind the belief?" When you get rid of that charge, your whole life will change.

No Requirements to Be Happy

Imagine that you are infinitely wealthy. That means that if you stopped working today, your passive income would be enough to live on for the rest of your life with your current lifestyle. What would you do? Would you continue to do the same work? Would you work to earn more passive income so that you could improve your lifestyle? Suppose you did that and your lifestyle became 10 times as affluent as it is now. Then what would you do? More of the same? Perhaps you'd work to give to others or to charity? Would you be happier if you were 10 times more affluent? Are you sure?

Once again let's look at the book by Jerry Stocking titled *Laughing with God*. As I've said, I have no idea whether God was involved in writing the material. However, the statements made are quite useful and stimulating, and that's enough for me. In that book, God says, *"If you cannot be perfectly content with nothing, you obviously cannot be content with anything."*

TAKE JOY IN THE SIMPLE THINGS

Although this might sound satirical to some of you, remember what we said before about having, doing, and being. Most people want to have what the good trader has (the money and success). Some are actually willing to do what the good trader does, taking a bigger step in the right direction. However, the real secret is to "be" the good trader. If you want to be happy or content or satisfied with your trading success, you have to be able to step into those states first. **Thus, the statement from God is perfectly logical. If you cannot be happy with nothing (i.e., just BE happy), you'll have trouble being happy as a result of some sort of doing or some sort of having.**

God goes on to say that *"the moment you focus on anything that you did not have at birth, you are deciding that you are somehow incomplete and can be fulfilled from outside of yourself."* Later He says, *"I put you in paradise, but you don't realize it, and you are attempting to improve on it."* This sort of approach does not work for the reasons I've just described.

God also says that our priorities are backward. That's probably nothing new and is easy to see in other people, although it's not always so easy to see in oneself. We tend to value what is rare. The less people have of something, the more valuable it tends to become. In contrast, God suggests that everything worth having is available in abundance. Everything we need is available in the proportion that we need it—things such as air, water, light, sunshine, and beauty. The most abundant thing we have is uncertainty, and we talked about how important it is in the last section. The markets would not be any fun if all that existed was certainty. In fact, most people would stop playing. Perhaps I should have put the word *playing* in italics because playing is what children do that gives them joy. As adults, we're taught to take life seriously and stop the joy.

Children take joy in the simplest things: walking through the woods, taking a deep breath of fresh air, being with someone who is fun, seeing a sunset, splashing in the rain. Adults tend to ignore all that wonderment. Instead, we work for money, security, and an improved lifestyle.

A long time ago I had a major goal to accumulate enough money to pay off my house. At that point, I felt I wouldn't have to work anymore. I knew I still would work, but it would be nice to be in a position in which I didn't have to. About 10 years ago, I fully began to understand the concept of infinite wealth as I explained it earlier. My passive income had to be greater than my expenses for me to be infinitely wealthy. Within six months I had became infinitely wealthy. Was I still doing the same things? Yes. Did I feel any different? Not really, except to the extent that I changed a lot about who I was "being" in order to become infinitely wealthy.

In *Laughing with God*, God says, "You have set up a world of unattainable goals—having the most or being the best. Those who come close will readily admit that there is nothing there worth attaining."

Here is an example of this logic that is worth thinking about:

You have a brand-new $250,000 car, and your neighbors do not have such a car. As a result, you must be more important than they are. Right? You must be good, successful, and important. Yet you don't spend much time joyriding in your $250,000 car because you don't want it to get dirty or damaged; mostly you just drive it a little to show people how important you are.

One day you decide to get in your car and take it for a long drive. You plan to drive 500 miles to a different state. However, when you're driving your expensive new car, you notice that you are tense and upset. Other drivers bother you. High-speed driving makes you tense. During the trip you get in a minor accident. Your car is badly dented, and you are miserable. Rather than laugh at the chance occurrence, you act as if it were you who was dented. Your value was in something else—your car. As a result, you've become vulnerable. You've confused yourself with your car, your boat, your house, whatever.

We have developed a value system in which we feel we earn something through hard work. We don't appreciate "things" unless we have suffered to obtain them. Making a difficult sale to an irate customer seems much more valuable than making an easy sale to a happy customer. We may celebrate the former and not think anything at all of the latter. All these values do is lead to hard work and irritation. We work overtime to get it done. Then we must spend time unwinding, usually by watching the television with a beer or a cigarette. What happened to simply enjoying life?

We invent substances that the average child would never want to consume or drink without being told it was "adult" to do so. The substances I'm talking about include beer, wine, whiskey, coffee, cigarettes, and cigars. We then invent "refined" tastes around these substances. Thus, people spend years learning about good wine, great coffee, or what a great cigar tastes like. Part of our enjoyment of life seems to lie in developing a refined sense of these substances (substances that the average child would never want to consume because they taste awful), and we consume them to unwind. Does that make sense to you?

What I'm saying may be true, but what does it have to do with good trading? Part of the reason I'm bringing these ideas to your attention is that most good traders can identify with what I'm talking about. They are into simplicity and the joy of life. That's part of what makes them good traders. When you can learn to "be" these things, you'll find that your trading will improve as a result of just being.

Let's continue with the idea that happiness comes from your "beingness," not from things or from what happens. As we just said, good traders are into simplicity and the joy of life. That's part of what makes them good traders, and when you can learn to "be" these things, you'll find that your trading will improve as a result.

What most of us really want are mental states such as joy, love, and freedom. To have those states, you need merely to step into them. They have nothing to do with what you have or do. Instead, they have everything to do with *being*. To raise the quality of your life, you need only look around you and rejoice. Are you having fun? Do you feel lighter? Are you experiencing more pleasure in the simplest things?

Reality, as it is described in *Laughing with God*, is all possibilities. It is absolute possibility. In fact, God says, *"All possibility is infinitely interesting, whereas some possibility is somewhat interesting, and one possibility is a problem."* In life, we get upset when we think that our possibilities have been limited, yet we also feel secure when we have certainty and possibilities are eliminated.

Someone asked me a question one day about all the bad news in the markets. It went something like this: "What is going to happen to the markets with the potential bear market, the devaluation of the dollar, and everything else that is going on? I find it a little scary, and it makes it hard to pull the trigger." What this person wants is one possibility—the markets going up. Yet the moment people feel that other possibilities are lost—for example, suppose someone says the markets will only go up—they act as if they've lost something or been robbed of something. What do you know? How can the markets only go up? We want the uncertainty that comes from not knowing.

A critical difference between good traders and average traders is that good traders thrive on simplicity and not knowing. They simply go with the flow of the markets. If the markets tell them it's time for stock prices to go up, they buy.

They may be wrong 60% of the time, but that is part of the game. They'll get out when the markets are no longer going up. They do this by simply observing what is happening and are joyful because they are going with the flow. They allow themselves to let their profits run because it's okay to be in the market when it is going up. They also allow themselves to get out because it's okay to get out when the markets start to do something else.

What I've just described is pure trading. Its essence is simple. It doesn't require a lot of time. Instead, it gives you lots of time to play. It also involves seeing all possibilities and being in the flow of what is happening right now. You cannot do this if you are preoccupied with being right, doing hard work, or having money or profits. You can do this only when your mind is pure and you can be at one with what is going on around you.

Try these simple tips:

1. Give up being right and embrace every possibility. You'll find that by not predicting the markets and enjoying the uncertainty, you are better able to observe what the markets are doing right now.

2. Add novelty to your life. Find five habits that you have and break them. If you put your trousers on with the right leg first, start with the left leg. If you listen to the phone with your right ear, pick it up with your left hand. Take two-plus hours to eat dinner and savor every bite. Go on a romantic holiday and make love in a new place every day in a different manner.

3. Pick several things that you do (especially in trading) and find a simpler way to do them. For example, if you are a day trader, open up a position and either take a loss or get out at the end of the day. When you do that, you are not tied to the market all day, and you may find that you take small losses and get huge profits. Simplify your entry technique and concentrate on exits. Or simplify both your entries and your exits and concentrate on position sizing.

4. Spend a full day doing absolutely nothing except meditating or walking outside.

5. Make a new friend and teach that person how joyous life can be. Pick someone who needs this lesson.

Vitamins for Your Soul to Improve Your Trading

Giving vitamins to your soul may not have a direct, noticeable effect on your bottom line. However, these vitamins could prevent a disaster and certainly will make you a lighter and happier person. Lighter and happier people usually make better traders and investors.

Several years ago, I began the year with a resolution to do a lot of spiritual work. I was planning to do a lot of meditation during January and February. I had a one-week spiritual retreat planned. In essence, this was the year to nurture my soul. Instead, what happened was that I spent December through February taking antibiotics for a bug that was resistant to antibiotics yet seemed to turn into chronic bronchitis or pneumonia because I initially ignored it. It was awful. It took all the energy out of me, and the last thing I wanted to do was a set of spiritual exercises or meditations.

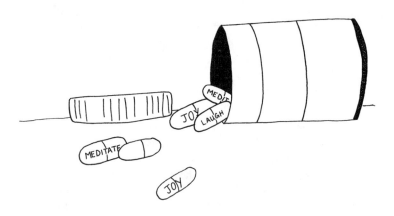

VITAMINS FOR YOUR SOUL

I believe in taking full responsibility for what happens to me. In most situations, I can explain exactly how I managed to create what has happened, but not for the first few months of that year. I honestly had no idea how I went from wanting to do spiritual work to going through physical exhaustion, but I did.

During that time I still had a strong urge to do things that might give my soul a charge—to feed it and nurture it. At the same time, I had no idea how to do that until the weekend I found a book called *Vitamins for the Soul.*[9] The book was just what I needed, but more important, it has helped me classify soul enrichment activities. Some of these activities I'm very strong in, but many of them are areas I've totally neglected.

Focus on the Moment

Mark Twain once said, "I've had many fears in my life, most of which never happened." So too, in my life I've noticed that I've had many worries, most of which never happened. Nevertheless, I can spend a lot of time being concerned about them. Yet the simplest solution is to concentrate on the opposite: What are your blessings, right now? What are you grateful for now?

Here are some interesting exercises you could do when the weather is nice just to concentrate on the wonders of this moment. Spend some time outside and really stretch your senses. Smell the flowers. Take in the smells and enjoy them. Close your eyes and listen to the sounds of nature. Hear the birds. Listen for the wind. What other animals do you hear? Take in the wonder of it all. Or go to a magnificent place and take in the scenery. What do you see? Look everywhere and take it all into your soul. Notice the magnificence of the moment.

Everything you think about is in the past. Even if you are feeling excruciating pain, what you actually are experiencing happened milliseconds ago. It's not what is happening now. Everything you think about and everything you worry about are in the past. When you release them and concentrate on the now, you'll find that everything is beautiful and peaceful. It's only our thoughts, based on our interpretations of what happened in the past, that cause upset and struggle. When you realize this, I believe that you'll have an enormous breakthrough in understanding who you really are.

Try this out: Take 15 minutes each day to enjoy the magnificence of the moment. Find something beautiful and take in the sights, sounds, smells, and so on. Notice how

---

[9] Sonia Choquette, *Vitamins for the Soul: Daily Doses of Wisdom for Personal Empowerment.* Carlsbad, CA: Hay House, 2005.

wonderful it all is and spend the full 15 minutes taking it in. When you are finished, give thanks. Notice what this does for your soul, how you feel, and ultimately your trading. You'll be surprised! Just try it.

Spend Some Time Laughing

Norman Cousins, the author of *Anatomy of Illness*,[10] believed that he cured himself of cancer by using laughter therapy. He found lots and lots of funny things and spent the day laughing and enjoying himself. The effect of changing his outlook to one of humor seemed to have immense healing effects on his body. However, there is no need to wait until you have a serious disease to practice taking vitamins for the soul.

I enjoy jokes and will laugh when something is funny, but I have not made a conscious effort to bring more laughter into my life. That's something I want to practice more.

Find some movies that are really funny and watch them. Better yet, invite some friends over and watch them together. There's only one rule for how to watch them: Laugh as much as you can. If something is a little funny, force yourself to laugh out loud. It's not that hard, and it's contagious. Also, save Internet jokes. You probably have friends who get lots of Internet jokes and would be happy to send them to you. I personally have at least four people who send me jokes all the time, and I save them. I can read through my old files any time I like, and some of the stuff is really funny. Get your friends to start sending you jokes (and send them jokes as well) and save your collection. Memorize them and tell them often. You'll find that when other people laugh at your joke collection, you'll laugh with them. Even though you know the joke and the punch line isn't a surprise, you'll get immense joy and fun from telling a joke to others.

Let me give you an example. About 10 years ago, one of my friends told a joke at dinner having to do with the three biggest lies a cowboy tells:

1. My truck is paid for.

2. I won this belt buckle at the rodeo.

3. I was just helping that sheep over the fence.

---

[10]Norman Cousins, *Anatomy of an Illness*. New York: Norton, 1979.

When my wife, who had just arrived from overseas and wasn't used to American humor, heard the joke, she didn't get the last lie at all, and the process of explaining it to her put everyone at the table in stitches. I don't even think the joke is that funny, but it's one I'll always remember because of my wife's reaction when it was being explained. Telling jokes to others can brighten up your soul. Practice doing it.

A healthy soul is a happy soul that experiences joy, laughter, and lightness. This doesn't mean that you must avoid looking at the suffering that occurs all around us, but it does mean that you avoid letting that suffering steal your joy over the many blessings God presents to us. The opposite of joy is not necessarily sorrow; it's unbelief in the true nature of your soul or the essence of God.

Many of us as adults have to relearn how to laugh, and that starts with a slight desire to do so. One of the amazing things about my wife is her laughter. She can laugh at almost everything, and I almost never hear her talking on the phone without hearing many bursts of laughter. It's one of the many reasons I'm so attracted to her. But the real secret of laughter is to just do it. If something is the least bit funny, try laughing at it even if it seems that you are forcing it at first. It becomes catching once you start.

Read something funny before you go to sleep each night. Get a collection of cartoon books or joke books and have them by your bedside. When something strikes you as the least bit funny, laugh out loud. You'll find that it is contagious and that the material becomes funnier and funnier.

Finally, you'll find that young children are much less inhibited about laughing than most adults are. Thus, spend time with kids and see what they think is funny. Go watch a movie or cartoon with them. Laugh when they laugh.

Here's your assignment with laughter for each day this week: Find something to laugh about each night before you go to sleep. In addition, watch a funny movie at least once a week this month. Enjoy it and have fun.

Give It to God

About nine years ago a traumatic event happened in my life; it changed a number of my values. It also caused me to worry a great deal—mostly over nothing—and spend a great deal of time feeling sorry for myself. Essentially, a lot of change happened in my life, mostly from as a result of my own internal creations, and I hated how my life was different and became very concerned about it.

Ironically, I spent four years going through *A Course in Miracles*[11] and learned that much of what we think of as reality is an illusion. I understood that what I created was an illusion and that I created it. Nevertheless, I worried about it constantly, even though nothing happened. My values changed and I stopped doing certain things that I used to do, yet nothing changed but the creation of new illusions.

Although much of what I've said in the prior two paragraphs may not make sense to you, perhaps it will when I give you the solution, the vitamin for the soul. My solution was to make a God Box. We keep this box in a special place in the house. Whenever something seems to really bother me, I do the following:

- First, I notice that I am spending a great deal of time in illusion and that it is not food for my soul.

- Once I've noticed the impact this item has on my life, I take a small piece of paper and write it down.

- As I write down what's bothering me, I give it to God.

- In addition, I give thanks to God, knowing that He will take it from me.

- I then put the piece of paper in my God Box and forget about it.

I've noticed that an amazing thing happens when I do this exercise. A problem that once dominated my thinking suddenly disappears. If it doesn't, the problem usually changes in some way and then I give the new problem to God the same way. To date, I've never had the same problem recur after I've offered it twice.

Occasionally, I might have a thought about the problem, but then I realize, "You just gave this to God. Are you now taking it back?" The answer is usually no, and I automatically drop it.

There is an interesting statement in *A Course in Miracles* that goes something like this: "*Everything is in God's control unless you have fear about it. When you have fear, you are*

---

[11]*A Course in Miracles.* Mill Valley, CA: Foundation for Inner Peace, 1975.

taking control away from God and trying to control the situation yourself through your own creations." Perhaps this explains why the God Box works so well. I strongly recommend this important vitamin for your soul. It works very well.

Practice this exercise for one week. Write down everything that bothers you. Even if you find yourself with a little irritation, just write it down on a piece of paper and put it in your God Box and then forget about it.

Give Thanks for Your Blessings

A great book that I recommend is called *The Marriage of Spirit*.[12] It's a whole program to help you lighten yourself, and part of the program is to keep a daily journal. When I did the program, I wrote down all the issues and emotional turmoil that I seemed to be going through that day. When I finished writing, I did exercises to clear out the turmoil.

What was interesting to me was noticing how much turmoil I could write down in that journal. The exercises seemed to work, but there was always something to write down. That surprised me since I've done hundreds of hours of personal clearing work over the years and thus expect to be pretty clear.

I remember an old adage that goes "You are what you think about." Actually, that's the law of attraction that you hear so much about these days. I'm very strongly in favor of personal clearing because most people have major scars on their souls that they need to heal. However, I'd cleared just about all of them as far as I knew, but I was still coming up with stuff.

Then it began to dawn on me how much time I was spending in my life looking for things to clear. When you look, you always find something. As a result, I changed my focus to giving thanks each day. Instead of looking for issues, I spent the same amount of time writing down the blessings in my life and giving thanks for those blessings. Quite often the blessings are the same ones, but that's okay because I'm still thankful for them.

I find that the process of writing down my blessings and giving thanks changes my focus entirely from the old process of finding my issues. What's occurred is a gradual lightening of my spirit. Again, this is a wonderful vitamin. Try it.

---

[12]Leslie Temple-Thurston and Brad Leslie, *The Marriage of Spirit: Enlightened Living in Today's World*. Santa Fe, NM: CoreLight, 2000.

Here's your assignment: Get a journal and each day write down five blessings you've experienced for which you are very grateful. In addition, if you find yourself worrying about anything or fearful about anything, write it down on a piece of paper and give it to God. Put it in your own God Box but remember that you have to be totally willing to turn it over to God and release it. If you don't give it willingly, you'll find that God is quite willing to let you keep it. *The Secret Gratitude Journal*[13] is an excellent vehicle for this purpose.

Follow Your Bliss

When I first went through *A Course in Miracles*, I made a commitment to follow my bliss. Joseph Campbell stated in his remarkable series *The Power of Myth*[14] that following your bliss is essentially following God's path. That seemed great to me: *Do what gives me joy, and my life will work better.*

In 1986, I made a commitment to quit my part-time job. I was working one day a week on a job I hated, but that job was a security blanket. As long as I was part-time, I had medical benefits and the possibility of working full-time again.

FOLLOW YOUR BLISS

[13]Rhonda Byrne, *The Secret Gratitude Journal*. New York: Atria Books, 2007.
[14]Joseph Campbell, *The Power of Myth*. New York: Doubleday, 1988.

I quit the job and got rid of the security blanket. Two weeks later my ex-wife unexpectedly lost her job and was not reemployed for about nine months. However, we made it through that year without having to borrow much money.

By 1987 my own business was progressing. I decided that I needed to hire a secretary to keep up with the workload. However, I hadn't made that much money the prior year, and a secretary's salary would take up most of that. Nevertheless, I took the plunge—another sign of commitment—and that year was the first year I made a six-figure salary. My business really seemed to take off from there.

In each case, the decisions were difficult. I was giving up security and the status quo for something unknown. Even though I hated the known and loved what I was going into, it was very scary. By the way, these are all steps to show commitment, and I've already talked about how important that is.

Along the way, through following this guidance about where joy seemed to be, I moved away from almost every attachment I had at the time, which included my first marriage. It wasn't working, and we couldn't seem to fix it. Much of this was very scary even though I was moving toward more joy. In the end, the results were wonderful. It's a big step, but following your bliss is a very important vitamin for your soul.

What do you love to do? You probably should be doing more of that. What do you hate to do? You probably should be doing less of that. At one point, when my business was already quite successful, I made a note of all the things I hated to do and all the things I loved to do. Guess what? All the things I loved to do were the things that made the most money for the business. They revolved around helping people, doing creative things, teaching my workshops, developing new products, and trading. Those were all things that made money.

I hated the day-to-day routine of managing the business and all the details that came with it. Although I still have some of those tasks, I have elected to find people who do a much better job with those things than I ever could. Now I concentrate totally on the things I love to do.

Make a list of what you love to do and what you dislike. If you love something, decide how you can do more of it. If you dislike something, determine how you can turn it over to someone else. You'll probably find that this simple act makes a tremendous difference in your life.

Commit to Love

I once attended a self-improvement workshop given by someone I considered very loving. Most of the workshop involved people bringing up problems, and he would lovingly help them release the problem. That was great, but I noticed that certain people would bring the same problem up over and over. In fact, one person, who might be described as a starving actor, had been to over 10 of those workshops and still was bringing up trivial stuff, almost as if he'd accomplished nothing. Nevertheless, the workshop guru laughed with him and gently took him through a release of his problem.

My initial thought was, "How can he not react to that person bringing up the same stuff over and over?" In fact, I'm sure he got in the workshop for free for being an assistant, but that means he probably brought up the same stuff over and over at each workshop. Then I thought, "How can he not react to this person's lack of progress?" Suddenly, he told me the secret. The secret was to love the person as he was. This means that he has no emotional investment in whether the person makes a change. He just loves the person, and that means he can respond lovingly no matter what happens. When I understood that, I really began to understand unconditional love.

This section is all about being loving. That means loving everything exactly as it is without making any judgments.

Most of our decisions are made from fear and worry. I can remember numerous times in the past when I might have noticed that a future workshop we were doing had a very low enrollment. My natural tendency would be to start to worry about that. What if no more people enroll? What if there are not enough enrollments to pay for speakers' fees, much less the hotel? But what if we cancel? Then we have a bad reputation with the hotel because they cannot rely on us. We also lose all the marketing money we've already spent on the workshop. I could go on and on with that kind of dialogue and worry. When I do that, I'm operating out of fear, and that's not useful. Instead, I elect to operate from love.

One way to operate out of love is to declare who you are. For example, you might make a declaration that says: "I'm a loving, kind, compassionate man." Write it out! Memorize it and declare it to yourself so that it becomes second nature to you. When you make decisions, you'll then begin to say,

"What does a loving, kind, compassionate man do in this situation?" He certainly doesn't make decisions that are based on fear. Instead, he bases decisions on love and compassion. Of course, the first thing that pops into my mind when I say that is "How can I handle this situation so that everyone wins?" What more can I give to increase enrollment in this workshop? How can I add more value to this workshop so that more people can attend? Of course, those responses get a much different response than I would get by saying, "We're going to lose a lot of money here even if I cancel the workshop."

Here's your next assignment: Decide who you are and make a commitment statement that reflects who you are. That statement might go something like this: "I'm a powerful, generous, kind leader!" or "I'm a courageous, loving, compassionate woman." Write down whatever you think might fit you. Put it on a sheet of paper and memorize it. When you make decisions, read your personal declaration and act as if it were true. Once you've done that, make your decision. If you do it that way, you'll probably find that your results are much different in all aspects of your life.

Meditate and Listen

When the day's activities have ended, take time to meditate. Or if you prefer, you might begin the day with meditation—whichever feels better for you. I believe meditating is very important. Here we'll just consider it as a soul vitamin.

Sit in an upright posture with your feet on the floor (if you're sitting in a chair) or your legs crossed (if you're sitting on the floor). Breathe slowly and notice the air going into your lungs and filling them. Notice where the air seems to go. In fact, you might want to control that by taking deep breaths and filling your lungs with air. Or perhaps you might want to allow your lungs to breathe by themselves as they have been doing for some time. Just notice what happens.

While you are noticing your breath, slow down or stop the chatter in your mind. Just concentrate on your breath. With practice, you'll get better and better at watching your breath. When you notice a lot of chatter going on, let it go and go back to watching your breath.

When you do this on a regular basis, you'll notice several things.

- First, you'll notice that you have a lot of chatter. That's great; just get it out of your system and allow yourself to quiet down. When stuff goes through your mind, notice that it's just the stuff of consciousness. It's not you at all; you are merely the awareness of that stuff going through your mind.

- Second, you might notice that you tend to fall asleep. If that's the case, great! You needed the sleep and get to refresh yourself with a little nap.

- You'll eventually notice that you are not the chatter in your head. Instead, you are the awareness of that chatter.

- Last, you might notice that you just slip into the space between your breaths.

NOTICE YOUR BREATHING

From this space come forth creativity, contact with higher realms of consciousness, and messages you may need to hear. Just listen. My recommendation is that you do this for about 20 minutes each day for an entire week. At a minimum, I think you'll find that when you do this for a week, you'll start to become more creative. The creative ideas may not happen while you are meditating, but you may find them flooding in at other times and may find that they help you become a better trader.

If you think about the essentials of life, the body can live without food for at least a month. You can do without water for several days, but you can do without air for only a few minutes. Air is absolutely essential for life, so why not promote it?

Many of the ancient meditation techniques involve the breath, and with good reason. Dr. Harry Goldbatt[15] found that rat cells deprived of oxygen easily developed malignancies whereas normal cells did not. Athletes, who get much more oxygen than other people do, have a cancer rate that is one-seventh the rate of the average American.

The lymphologist Jack Shields[16] has shown that deep diaphragmatic breathing is the most effective way to stimulate and clean the lymphatic system and actually stimulates the immune system. Deep breathing multiplies the rate at which the body eliminates toxins.

I'd like to extend this information and suggest that healthy breathing, enough to stimulate the immune system, not only prevents disease but actually improves performance. I suggest that you do the following exercise: At least once each day, take 10 deep breaths.

Breathe in the following manner: Inhale for five seconds, starting the breath deep in your abdomen with your diaphragm. Now hold that breath for 20 seconds to help it oxygenate your blood and activate your lymphatic system. Finally, breathe out for 10 seconds.

---

[15]Harry Goldblatt and Gladys Caeron. Induced malignancy in cells from rat myocardium subjected to intermittent anerobiosis during long propagation in vitro. *Journal of Experimental Medicine*, 97(4): 525–552.

[16]Clydette Clayton, http://www.articlesbase.com/health-articles/why-deep-breathing-for-fast-back-pain-relief-582458.html.

If this exercise is too strenuous, use a smaller number in the ratio 1:4:2. In other words, hold for four times as long as you inhale. Try this exercise twice a day for the next month and note how you feel.

Chances are, if you commit to it, you'll find yourself becoming a littler clearer, a little more open, and a little more receptive to what is really happening. If that happens, even if you are only slightly aware of it, you should notice a difference in your trading. However, all this assumes that you are following some of the other ideas in this book.

By the way, the Hindus have developed an extensive set of breathing exercises designed to help the body and soul. These are called Pranayama exercises and Pranakriya exercises. If you like this one, consider researching these exercises and doing more.

Around 1990 I worked with a retired professor of engineering. We did some clearing work together, and at the end of that task I taught him how to follow his internal guidance. His internal guidance took him a long way over the next 18 years, and I again found myself working with him, only this time I was doing spiritual work under his guidance.

However, what impressed me the most was the purity with which he could watch the market and still do what it was telling him to do. This means he'd buy what was going up and sell it when it stopped going up. He'd also sell short what was going down and buy it back when it stopped going down. Over the 18 years his account had grown big enough to be a substantial hedge fund. All his money was earned through trading simple principles. Don't dismiss the value of vitamins for your soul.

Discipline in Meeting Your Goals

You should now have some specific goals in your trading. If you don't, I suggest that you develop some. However, even if you do, you may need some discipline to help you meet those goals. As a result, I thought I'd focus on helping you meet your goals.

1. Divide a General Goal into Specific Steps

Most trading goals are huge. As a result, I'd suggest that you divide a goal into specific steps. It's much easier to accomplish small steps that you can imagine doing for the rest of the year (or the rest of your life) than it is to fulfill a giant goal. Start with something that is easy and make sure you can accomplish it.

A resolution to make 50% this year in your account could be broken into a number of steps such as the following: (1) Look at ideas that might help improve your trading, (2) test each idea and see how much improvement you will get from it, and (3) implement the best idea by following the top tasks of trading. In fact, your resolution might simply be to follow the top tasks of trading each day and notice what that means for you. Many of those tasks are mentioned throughout this book. By the way, if you risk 1% per trade, you only need to make 1R per week to have a 50% return.

2. Make Promises to Yourself and Include the Reason for a Promise in the Resolution

Suppose your promise to yourself is to do a daily mental rehearsal, one of the tasks of top trading. The way you might phrase that is to promise yourself to do a daily mental rehearsal to plan ways to increase your discipline. The second statement is much easier for you to follow through with on a regular basis. Also make sure that the promise you set is something you want to do and not something someone else wants you to do. If I tell you that you must do a daily mental rehearsal, you are not likely to do it. In contrast, if you decide how important this kind of rehearsal will be for your well-being and your trading, you are much more likely to do it.

3. Determine Your Triggers

If you are setting a resolution, it is probably because you want to do something you have not been able to do. There is probably a reason for your inability to do it, certain triggers that set you off. What are those triggers? Are there environmental triggers, such as the presence of certain people or certain conditions? Are there certain internal feelings that set you off? What are those feelings, and when do they occur?

Once you determine your triggers, you are much more prepared for them. I strongly recommend doing extensive mental rehearsal around the issue of dealing with those triggers. Awareness is a big part of keeping your resolutions.

4. Look at the Positive Side of Your New Goal

When we get into the act of keeping our resolutions, we sometimes feel that we are denying ourselves. Instead, look at the positive side of what you are accomplishing. Turn on something positive. For example, if you are trying to stop taking trades that have nothing to do with your system, concentrate on the joy of following your system and making money. Concentrate on the joy of the new behavior instead of the negative thing you are trying to overcome. You'll find that moving forward is much easier.

5. Keep a Diary of Whatever It Is You Are Working On

A lot of what I've suggested involves mental awareness. Most people are unaware of the big picture that's involved in accomplishing a goal. However, when you keep a diary that lists your accomplishments and your thoughts, you'll find it much easier to understand what is going on inside of you.

Listing your accomplishments is also a form of reward. When you focus on your accomplishments—especially if you've followed step 1 and set small steps toward your total goal—you'll feel great about what you achieved and where you are going.

6. Make It Okay to Give in Occasionally

If you are attempting to make a major change, you may have occasional setbacks. If you view a setback as a failure, the resolution is over. You can give yourself a bad name. In contrast, if you make it okay to have occasional setbacks, you can keep going—it's just a setback.

Realize that a setback is an opportunity to learn something about yourself. What happened? What were your thoughts? Write down all that information in your diary and determine what you can learn from it. You may discover a new trigger, and then you can make a plan for getting around that and other triggers. In any case, forgive yourself for the setback and move on.

Quite often setbacks are due to inadequate preparation. Perhaps you didn't do enough research with respect to your trading. Perhaps more mental rehearsal was needed. Perhaps you discovered something about your thought process that you didn't expect but now can use in your preparation. What additional preparation can you do to make sure you move ahead toward generally keeping your resolution?

7. Reward Yourself throughout the Process

You need to acknowledge accomplishments early in the process. The first few days will probably be the hardest. Consequently, when you get through those days and accomplish your goals, find a reward. Make the process fun through a system of rewards.

Removing Stored Charge

We talked about the Belief Examination Paradigm earlier in this book and how charge (stored feelings) will cause you to keep limiting beliefs because the charge gives a belief energy. Now it's time to remove some of that charge. Let's say you've done the belief exercise at least 100 times. You've come up with a list of common charges attached to a number of your beliefs:

- Fear
- Anger
- Rejection
- Guilt
- Loneliness
- Uncertainty
- Losing control
- Abandonment

What do you do with this list?

First, let's look at why we store feelings in the body. We judge a feeling to be good or bad. We are willing to feel the good feelings but are not willing to feel the bad ones. This probably was conditioned by your parents, who said things like this: "Big boys like you shouldn't be afraid" and "If you do that again [express anger], I'll really give you something to be angry over."

The net result is that we attempt to suppress negative feelings. For example, the hero in action movies doesn't show his or her emotions. Heroes just stuff their emotions and get on with their lives, and you probably learned to admire such persons.

Now let's look at what might happen when you stuff an emotion inside that you are not willing to feel. For example, suppose you see an attractive person and you go up to meet him or her. This person has nothing against you, but he or she has had a bad day. As a result, his or her reaction to you is "Get lost! I'm not interested."

You feel rejected. You don't like the feeling, and you stuff it away (you are not willing to feel it). You probably mumble something such as the following: "I didn't want to go out with him or her anyway."

What happens now is that you have stored rejection in your body. Also, you've probably created a part of you that doesn't want to feel rejection again. In fact, its job is to never again feel rejected.

A week later you see another attractive person you want to approach. You start to move toward that person, and suddenly this part of you says, "Remember what happened last week," and it releases a little of the stored rejection. The new person has done nothing, but you already feel rejected. However, you approach him or her, and that part keeps warning you and releasing more stored rejection.

One result might be that you give up and never approach the person, feeling that the possibility of rejection is so strong that you don't want to take a chance. But remember that this second person has not even seen you or reacted to you. You are just reacting to what might happen.

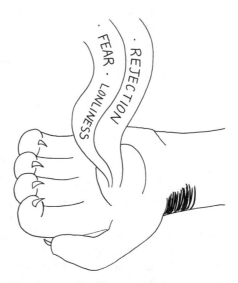

LET GO OF NEGATIVE EMOTIONS

The second possibility is that you approach the person anticipating rejection, saying something like the following: "You wouldn't want to go out with me, would you?" This approach almost guarantees rejection, and you get to be right about it. Now rejection is a permanent part of your experience unless you do feeling release on it.

I know of three feeling release exercises that are fine for you to do right now:

- Welcoming the feeling
- Just releasing it
- The park bench exercise

Think about one of the beliefs you'd like to get rid of but cannot. Let's say there is some rejection involved in that belief. It's charged with rejection. Think about the belief and releasing it. When you notice rejection coming up, welcome it. Open your arms wide and just welcome the feelings you have. I personally find this exercise to be quite powerful. Feelings are meant to pass through you, not be stored inside you.

The second exercise amounts to releasing the feelings as they come up. Just feel it and let it go. It's that simple.

Actually, the only time it is difficult is when you resist doing it. The resistance magnifies the feeling, and you then have to deal with the resistance. If the feeling seems like a category 5 hurricane, it means you are resisting it strongly. Notice that you are resisting it; then just welcome it and let go of the resistance. Once you have done that, releasing the feeling should be easy.

I strongly recommend that you take the Sedona Method Course,[17] which includes 20 CDs on feeling release. It covers these methods and quite a few more.

I advocate using the third method—the park bench technique—when a feeling you are resisting is dominating your life. Let's say a loved one died and you are preoccupied with grief. Let's say you are spending 15 hours a day grieving over your loss. If this is happening, I recommend the park bench technique, in which you actively commit to the feeling. You are spending 15 hours a day with it, so why not commit one hour each day to really feel the feeling?

---

[17]Hale Dwoskin, *The Sedona Method: Your Key to Lasting Happiness, Success, Peace, and Emotional Well-Being.* Sedona, AZ: Sedona Press, 2003.

Find a neutral spot, such as a park bench. Sit down on the bench and commit to feeling the feeling as strongly as you can for one hour. What you'll find is that you probably can do it for 20 minutes, but then the feeling gets boring and starts to dissipate. However, you must do it for an hour. After the first day you may find that you are not thinking about it so much.

The next day you decide to spend 45 minutes on the bench thinking about the feeling. And after 15 minutes it gets boring, but you must do the whole 45 minutes.

The next day you reduce it to 30 minutes, then to 20, then to 10, and then down to 5 minutes. Pretty soon it seems to go away instantly, and you are not thinking about it all day. Why does this happen? It happens because you've been willing to feel it actively.

Now look at the beliefs you want to change that have a charge on them. Practice one or more of the feeling release techniques just recommended on the charge behind those beliefs. Pretty soon, the charge will be gone from the nonuseful beliefs and you'll simply be able to replace them all with much more useful beliefs.

How Do You Know When You've Done Enough Self-Work?

In my experience no one solves all of his or her personal issues. Working on oneself is a lifelong task, and when you get through one area, another one usually appears. If you've never solved or even recognized an issue of self-sabotage, the first one you deal with will have a major impact on you. When you get through the first major issue and know it's finished, the feeling is tremendous. You know you've accomplished something major, perhaps something you've been working on for a long, long time.

My belief is that once you've worked through five major areas, you are generally a changed person. Furthermore, I have faith that you will continue to work on yourself and be able to deal with anything else that gets in the way of your goals.

Here are some examples of what people have said after working through a major issue.

Example 1 (good answer): I have noticed that whenever I feel stressed and out of harmony with the universe, I am acting out of fear. That fear may be related to being liked, feelings of unworthiness, or fear of making mistakes, but it is unimportant what the fear is related to. The fact that a decision is based on fear puts it out of harmony with the universal order, whereas decisions based on love increase that harmony. To tell the difference and make a decision that is based on love, I need to notice the way my body feels when the decision is being made. If my body reflects feelings of tension, anger, or irritation, I am acting out of fear. If my body reflects feeling of relaxation, well-being, or harmony, I am acting out of love. I am trying to increase my attention to this before the decision is implemented.

Here is an even better example.

Example 2 (excellent answer): I am working on insecurity, fear of failure, and fear of loss, which I believe are related and which I'll collectively refer to as insecurity. This has been a difficult issue for me to realize existed and work on, but as I've worked on it and other issues, it has become easier to deal with.

I have used a variety of approaches toward insecurity, one of which has been to look back over my life to see where the insecurity comes from; I didn't have a deprived, unloving childhood. Nevertheless, I have been able to recollect insecurity being an influence on my behavior in a variety of situation over many years. For certain situations that I didn't handle well, I've gone back in my mind to recollect what I was thinking and feeling to analyze my emotional state. I've replayed the situations in my mind a number of different ways to show myself how they could have been better and why my insecurity was unjustified and a hindrance.

I have been a very successful professional. I think my insecurity has, in part, been a driver for my worldly successes and has influenced me to undertake new, major challenges in my life. Fear of failure or loss has motivated me to do well in situations in which excellent performance was needed and expected by third parties such as clients. However, it also has caused me to refuse to recognize that a situation has soured and requires a change in action. I have had to learn to tell myself that it's okay to lose (or fail) at something, to cut my losses and move on.

I believe these insecurity issues are bound up with self-esteem issues, and so I have been working more and more on self-esteem. As I have done so, I have felt much better able to deal with the insecurity issues. This is the case because I have found that self-esteem issues, if they are recognized and acknowledged, are somewhat difficult but tractable. I have gone through several periods of change in my life and in the way I think about myself. I find the process hard but manageable. For me, it requires stepping outside myself and trying to view myself as others may see me. It also involves putting any situation in which I have reacted insecurely in perspective.

When someone has gone through five major issues that he or she can explain in this manner, I know that person can handle anything.

Here are two examples of unacceptable answers I've see that reflect shallow self-awareness.

Unacceptable example 1: My marriage is a major issue. My spouse and I effectively separated and then decided to reunite, but the result was not satisfactory to me. As a result, I found a counselor and persuaded my wife to begin counseling.

The counselor likes us and my spouse likes him, and so we seem to have established a stable counseling relationship. However, I don't feel the marriage has improved at all, and I don't have an image of how counseling will help. However, I trust the process because the counselor is very experienced and because I don't know any alternative.

My response to this answer: What's wrong with the marriage? What are the issues involved? How do they reflect what's going on inside you? The answers to these questions may be acceptable responses for several areas you are working on.

Unacceptable example 2: Health and diet is where it all starts. The quality of the substances you put in your body is equal to the quality of energy, decisions, and actions you get out. When I've taken the time to nourish my body properly, the level of focus that becomes available is very high. Ideas flow, and being creative comes easily.

My response to this answer was: This is a statement of beliefs; it reflects very little internal awareness. If there is a struggle with diet (i.e., because of a feeling of being deprived when you can't have something or similar types of feelings), that may be an area you are working on.

I hope you can see the difference. Now ask yourself, "What are five major issues I have had in my life? How did I produce those issues, and how did I make them nonissues?" When you can answer this question from a position of transformation, it's safe to move on. Otherwise, continue working.

PART 2

Developing a Business Plan: Your Working Guide to Success in the Markets

Have a Plan for Your Trading/Investing

What happens when someone gives you a tip or idea about the market? Do you get excited about it and want to act on it? Do you become skeptical and suddenly distrust the person who gave you the tip? In some cases you probably act and in other cases you become skeptical, possibly depending on the source.

HAVE A PLAN FOR YOUR TRADING

A better alternative is to notice whether the tip fits into your business plan for trading. If it fits, you then do more evaluation in accordance with the criteria you use in your plan. If it does not fit, you simply discard it, saying, "That's not something I know much about."

The only correct response to a "hot tip" is to integrate it into your business plan for trading. If it does fit and suggests that you do more evaluation, fine. That's a proper response.

An improper response is to go out and buy an exchange-traded fund (ETF) of Japanese stocks just because some guru recommended it.

This suggestion constitutes a test for your plan. Do you have a plan that helps you deal with "new surefire can't lose" tips you've heard about? If you do not, perhaps it's time you developed one. This means developing a thorough business plan to guide your trading. Do whatever it takes to develop a thorough business plan to cover your trading or investing.

Here's a brief outline for what needs to be incorporated into your business plan. This outline is for individuals who are trading or investing for themselves; those of you who are running a trading business need something much more elaborate.

1. What's your mission statement? What's the real motivation behind your trading?

2. What are your goals and objectives? You cannot get from A to B easily unless you know where B is.

3. What are your trading and market beliefs? You cannot trade the market. You can only trade your beliefs about the market. As a result, it's a good idea to know what those beliefs are.

4. What is the big picture that affects the world markets, and do you have specific trading plans that fit that big picture?

5. What is your tactical trading strategy, and what is its expectancy? What setups do you use before entry? What is your timing signal for entry? What is your worst-case loss going to be, and how is it determined? How will you take profits? What is the expectancy of that methodology? We deal with this topic in Part 3 of this book.

6. What is your plan for position sizing (the part of your methodology that tells you "how much" throughout the course of a trade)? We deal with this topic in Part 4 of this book.

7. What are your typical psychological challenges and problems in following this plan? What is your plan for psychological management for dealing with these problems?

8. What are your daily procedures?

9. What is your education plan? How do you plan to improve yourself continuously?

10. What is your disaster plan? What can go wrong, and how will you deal with each item?

11. What is your planned income and budget for expenses? Are they realistic?

12. What other types of systems are important for you, and how will you plan for them? Examples are keeping your data accurate, explaining results to clients or family, doing research, and keeping track of your trades and your accounting. These are all important.

13. How do you relate to business systems:

- As someone who just needs to be told what to do?

- As someone who is the system and becomes a perfectionist?

- As someone who develops systems so that others can do the work?

- As someone who invests in systems?

14. How do you prevent mistakes and avoid repeating them if they occur? This is the topic of Part 5 of this book.

Having a plan of this nature is so important that I rank it among my top requirements for traders. Perhaps it's time you developed such a plan.

Having a Mission Statement behind Your Trading Is Critical to Your Success as a Trader

You probably have specific goals in your trading. If you don't, I suggest that you develop some. Surely Part 1 of this book gave you some ideas. Once you have goals, you may need some discipline to help you meet them. As a trader, you need a mission statement to form the core of that discipline.

I once spent several days doing creative brainstorming on ways to take my company to the next level. Part of that process involved determining our mission statement. I'd always known what our mission was, but I'd never put it down on paper. I also had not thought about our expansion with respect to that mission. It's a critical process and one you should do with your trading. It also fits with the overall idea that you must understand who you are and who you want to be before developing a business because your business will develop out of your statement about who you want to be.

In the brainstorming process, I learned a technique that works for running any successful business. When I thought about it, it was obvious that it was a technique that is applicable to trading. The first part of it is to create a mission statement for your trading business. Here are a few examples of what that statement could be for you:

- Help others to prosperity by becoming a highly successful money management firm.
- Build a hedge fund with at least $250 million under management.
- Produce an infinite wealth stream (enough passive income to meet my expenses) within five years.
- Be a vehicle for me to grow moneywise and as a person.
- Fund a charitable foundation.
- Help others grow as traders by transforming themselves.

Second, you need to evaluate new projects with respect to the mission statement. When you have a mission statement, you can evaluate new projects (or new systems) constantly with respect to that statement by asking, "Is my objective in this project critical to the mission of the company?" People are always asking me to do this project or that project. For example, one trader, who was a sound engineer by training, said that when he came into town, we could start working on developing specific meditations for traders. Although his idea was a great one, it was very low on my list of mission-critical tasks that needed to be done in the near future. As a result, it didn't happen. Without such a process in place, I'd probably spend most of my time doing noncritical tasks and thus not accomplishing what is important for the company to meet its goals.

Most traders treat their trading business like a hobby; in other words, they don't treat it seriously. For example, some constantly look for new or better systems. Others trade discretionarily. Still others manage the money of a few friends or relatives without thinking of the consequences. These types of objectives need to be evaluated with respect to your trading mission statement to see how they fit.

Let's make the assumption that you have a mission statement for your trading business to produce an infinite wealth stream for yourself within five years. Infinite wealth basically means that if you stopped working, including working at your trading business, you would have enough passive income (i.e., your money working for you) to maintain your current lifestyle. You could accomplish this in two ways. First, you could accumulate enough money that if you invested it in T-bills or some other form of passive investment (I'd recommend a good hedge fund over T-bills because you can get a much better rate of return), you'd be infinitely wealthy. Second, you could automate your systems for trading so much that you could hire someone else to execute the trades for you.

Let's take a look at some of the objectives we introduced to see if they fit with this mission statement.

Let's Try This New System to See If It Works Better

If you have a system already that can help you achieve this goal, you probably are just wasting your time. For example, I've known people with systems that can easily net 100% or more each year who constantly jump on the next new system that comes along. However, if you don't have a system that will meet your objectives, you need to evaluate both your current system and the new one in terms of R-multiples, expectancy, opportunity, and the concepts involved to see if you have something that logically makes sense. For example, if you assume that you will risk 1% per trade, you have to net only about 8R per month (remember that R refers to your risk in each trade) to make 100% per year. Think about it. In most cases, someone else's new system will not help you because that person has not evaluated it in these terms. It usually takes only a slight change in your thinking to net you great rates of returns. Thus, looking at a new system is probably a total waste of time in light of this mission statement.

I Want to Make Discretionary Trades Because I Think I Can Outperform a Mechanical System

This objective might fit within the mission of infinite wealth if your plan is to accumulate a certain amount of money and then invest it in various forms of passive income to produce infinite wealth. However, if you plan to produce infinite wealth through your own trading, it does not fit within the objectives because you will always be tied to your trading: You will always have to work if you make discretionary trades. In the second case, you should abandon the idea of discretionary trading.

I'll Manage Money for a Few Friends and Relatives

This objective could be a total distraction for your mission or it could be a means to an end, depending on how you treat the practice of managing money. For example, are you going to do it for free or charge a fee? If you plan to charge a fee, that could help you meet a monetary target. However, are you prepared to deal with the psychology of the people for whom you are managing money? Do you have back office accounting procedures in place? Is the effort to deal with accounting and your clients worth the distraction to your trading? If the answer to any of these questions is no, this is not a mission-critical objective and should be abandoned on the spot.

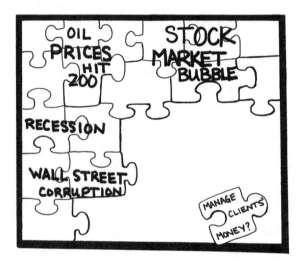

HOW DOES EACH PIECE FIT THE BIG PICTURE?

If the project is mission-critical, you need to allocate human and capital resources to it. Let's make the assumption that your idea seems to be mission-critical. Let's say that your mission is to open a hedge fund with a target of at least $250 million under management and some friends are asking you to manage their money. To have large amounts of money under management, you need to produce above-average returns with very little risk. For example, a system that would help you achieve this mission would be one that would earn 15% to 25% each year with no more than one or two losing months a year. If you have that kind of system in place, accepting clients' money probably would be useful. If you don't have such a system in place, client money probably would be a major distraction. Let's say you have the system in place and decide to accept money.

The next step is to determine the human and capital resources you need to allocate before undertaking the step of accepting client money. What else do you need to have in place before accepting client money? First, you have to have accounting systems in place. If you don't, you need to (1) find someone to help you with your accounting and (2) put a system in place to report to clients. This amounts to allocating either human or capital resources to your objective.

Second, you need to have systems in place for dealing with client inquiries (including new clients). How will you market to clients? How will you deal with clients who want information about their accounts or about your trading? Again, since you have decided that accepting client money is mission-critical, you need to allocate human and capital resources to putting these systems in place.

Next, you need a timeline for the project. If you decide that the project is mission-critical and have allocated resources to it, you have to have a timeline for the completion of the project. Without a timeline, you could go on forever with the project.

Finally, you need a feedback and monitoring process for the project. This process will keep you on track and prevent you from wasting resources. When you allocate resources to a project that is mission-critical for your trading business, have a way to monitor its progress. How will you know that resources are being spent properly? How will you know that progress is satisfactory? If someone else is involved, how will you know that that person is doing a good job? These are key tasks to perform if your trading business is to accomplish its mission.

What Are Your Goals and Objectives?

You cannot get from A to B easily unless you know the location of B. Most people don't think too much about their objectives: what kinds of returns they want or what kinds of drawdowns they are willing to accept. However, you cannot develop any sort of trading system, at least one that you'll be happy trading, without knowing these things. For example, you may decide that you want to make at least 20% and have a peak-to-trough drawdown of no more than 10%. That's a reasonable objective, but it's totally different from the objective of someone who wants to make as much money as possible and not worry about drawdowns at all. Those two objectives would have entirely different position sizing methods to get there.

Let me illustrate how many possible objectives you could have.

First, you might want to maximize your probability of achieving a certain goal. That goal could be anything from making a profit to making 1,000% or more.

Second, you might want to make sure that you don't have a drawdown of a certain size from your peak equity. That drawdown could be anything from, say, 2% to 100%.

Third, you might want to minimize your probability of losing a certain percentage of your starting equity at the beginning of the year. For example, you might be willing to have a large peak-to-trough drawdown, but you might want to minimize the chances of losing more than a small amount of your starting equity. That could be 1% up to, say, 75%.

Fourth, you might want to achieve the highest possible equity at the end of the year and maximize your chances of achieving that goal.

Fifth, you might want to maximize the probability of having the greatest chance of meeting your goal and the smallest chance of experiencing your worst-case drawdown.

When you consider that it's possible to put many numbers into these objectives, it is easy to see how each trader/investor can have different objectives. In fact, there are probably as many objectives as there are traders.

What are those objectives for you? Deciding on your objectives is about 50% of developing a trading system. Developing a system without an objective becomes an insane exercise, although many people do that.

Market Beliefs

When you trade, you probably think you trade the markets. However, you don't trade the markets; instead, you trade your beliefs about the markets.

What do I mean when I say, "We only trade our beliefs about the markets"?

Let's look at some statements and see what you believe about them:

THE MARKET IS A DANGEROUS PLACE!

- The market is a dangerous place in which to invest. (You are right.)

- The market is a safe place in which to invest. (You are right.)

- Wall Street controls the markets, and it's hard for the little guy. (You are right.)

- You can easily make money in the markets. (You are right.)

- It's hard to make money in the markets. (You are right if you really believe that.)

- You need to have lots of information before you can trade profitably. (You are right.)

Do you notice the theme? You are right about every one of these beliefs whether you said yes or no to any of them. If you don't believe in any of these statements, what do you believe instead? You are right about that, too! However, there is no real right or wrong answer. Some people will have the same beliefs and agree with you, and others won't. Therefore, whatever your beliefs are about the markets, they will direct your thinking and your subsequent actions.

Let's look at one concept that works: trend following. To be a good trend follower, you must start by identifying something that is in a trend. Once you've done that, you must jump on the trend, perhaps after a retracement. Note that I've made two statements about trend following. Both of those statements are beliefs; they are not necessarily true. They are simply my way of organizing reality for myself. A lot of people (i.e., other trend followers) may share that reality, but it's still based on a couple of beliefs.

You could have beliefs that would make it very difficult to be a trend follower:

- The stock just made a new high. How could I possibly buy a stock that has made a new high?

- Trend following works for some people, but when I get in at a new high, that's likely to be the turning point in the market.

- Whenever I enter the market, it's a signal to Wall Street to do the opposite of what I just did.

- Momentum trading doesn't work; you have to buy value.

- The stock market doesn't trend very well; it tends to be very choppy.

Note that these are all beliefs. Yet how could you be a trend follower if you believed any of these things? Are you beginning to see how beliefs shape your trading behavior?

Let's look at another method that works: value trading. To be a value trader, you probably have to have one or more of the following beliefs:

- When I buy things that are undervalued, with patience they will move toward fair value and I'll make money.
- When I buy things that are undervalued, they eventually will become overvalued, and that's when I should sell.
- Something is undervalued when . . .
- Something is overvalued when , , ,

There are many successful value investors, but you probably couldn't be a value trader if you believed that things must be moving rapidly in your favor for you to make money. Also, if you buy undervalued stocks, it can take forever to make a profit, but you want to make money each day.

My purpose in getting you to explore your beliefs about the market is to show the major influences on the way you trade. Write down your beliefs about the market and the way you should trade. You have not completed this exercise until you've written down 200 or more beliefs. If you find this difficult, try looking at charts and predicting what will happen next.

Your beliefs may fall into the following categories:

- What do I believe about the market?
- What do I believe about trading?
- What trading concepts do I believe work?
- What risk management principles work?
- How do the best traders trade?
- Who are some of the best traders, and what do they believe that I believe?
- What are the secrets to making money in the markets?
- What have I read lately about trading that resonates with me?
- When I try to predict what a stock will do from a chart, what concepts come up for me?

To give you a sample, here is a list of my beliefs, one from almost every category:

1. I believe we are in a long bear market in which market valuations (price/earnings ratios) will go down to the single-digit range.

2. I believe that whenever you enter a trade, you must know the point at which you are willing to say, "I was wrong about this trade" and get out. This is your stop loss point.

3. I like to trade stocks that are very efficient (i.e., moving up with very little volatility).

4. Sometimes there are a lot of efficient stocks to select from, and sometimes one cannot find any.

5. When you get stopped out of a trade, make sure (if you can) that you don't lose more than 1% of your equity in that trade.

6. The best traders trade by finding a niche that fits them and then becoming an expert in that niche.

7. One of the secrets to making money is to have well-thought-out objectives and then understand that you meet those objectives with position sizing.

8. What have I read about trading lately that resonates with me? I just noticed a Warren Buffett quote: "Diversification is a substitute for not thinking."

Each belief fits me. They may not fit you at all; however, I believe that you'll have trouble as a trader/investor if you ignore some of those beliefs (i.e., the second, fifth, sixth, and seventh). But that's another story. Anyway, your job is to now write down 10 to 15 beliefs from each category.

When you've finished the exercise, look over each belief and run it through the Belief Examination Paradigm:

- Who gave me the belief—where did it come from?
- What does this belief get me into? List at least five things.
- What does this belief get me out of? List at least five things.

- Is this belief useful, or is there a more useful belief?

- Does this belief limit me?

- How could I change it so that it is less limiting?

- If I can't change it, is there a charge on the belief?

- If it's appropriate, ask questions such as, "How do I define that?" and "How do I know?"

My work in modeling top traders suggests that if you are to do well, you must have a trading system that fits you. By writing down your beliefs, you are well on your way to developing a trading system that does that.

Understanding the Big Picture

I've been in business as a trading coach for over 25 years, and during that time I've seen many "trends" in investors. I've seen a commodities boom, a forex boom, an equities boom, a day-trading boom, and even a total disaster period in which there was a boom only in things that one might short. Because of this, I think it is very important for people to be aware of the big picture. The big picture will tell you what's going on and at least make you aware that what you are doing could end suddenly. In fact, it usually ends when you are most excited about it.

I would like my clients to endure and not be a part of these trends when the bubble bursts. As a result, in Chapter 6 of the second edition of my book *Trade Your Way to Financial Freedom*, I presented six major factors that I believe influence the big picture:

1. **Factor 1: The U.S. Debt Situation.** The interest on the "official" debt of the U.S. government is now equal to the nation's annual deficit. The debt situation is more interesting than one might think, and there are some serious questions you must ask yourself. Did you know that the Federal Reserve Bank of St. Louis has published a study saying that the United States is bankrupt?[1]

UNDERSTANDING THE BIG PICTURE

---

[1]research.stlouisfed.org/publications/review/06/07/Kotlikoff.pdf.

2. **Factor 2: The Secular Bear Market.**[2] The U.S. stock market has had secular cycles (long-term cycles that last 15 to 20 years) throughout its existence. These are not stock price cycles but cycles in the price/earnings (P/E) ratios of stock prices. A bear cycle started in 2000 and could last until 2020. Again, there are some serious issues here that you need to familiarize yourself with as a trader/investor.

3. **Factor 3: The Globalization of the Economy.** The fastest-growing economy in the world is now China, and India is making immense strides as well. China is consuming vast amounts of raw materials, and this has had some interesting economic effects on the world. As a trader/investor, there are some important questions you need to ask yourself about this factor. When the economy collapsed in 2008, everything collapsed.

4. **Factor 4: The Impact of Mutual Funds.** To understand the potential impact of future events on the U.S. economy, it's important to understand the role of mutual funds and the ways their managers think. Mutual funds certainly do not follow any of the principles of trading outlined in *Trade Your Way to Financial Freedom,* and you need to think about the impact of this and some of the things that are going to happen in the future. In 1982, when the great secular bull market started, there were only a few mutual funds. When it ended in 2000, there were more mutual funds than listed stocks. My prediction is that very few funds will be able to withstand the secular bear market with their philosophy of being 100% invested. Thus, when a new secular bull market starts, there again will be very few mutual funds. Perhaps this time they'll be allowed to go to cash.

5. **Factor 5: Changes in Rules, Regulations, and Policies.** Sometimes trader trends such as day trading are ended suddenly by changes in regulations that are designed to "protect" the investor.

---

[2]Michael Alexander, *Stock Cycles: Why Stocks Won't Beat Money Markets over the Next Twenty Years.* Lincoln, NE: iUniverse, 2000.

6. **Factor 6: Human Beings Tend to Play a Losing Economic Game.** If you really understand this factor, your chances of long-term success in the market are greatly increased. But do you know that the big players have a different set of rules than you do? You cannot play by their rules, and if you trade the way they do, you are probably doomed. As a result, there are some serious questions you need to ask yourself. Most of the big players do not understand risk; they just think they do. That is why banks have rogue traders. It is why banks are leveraged 30 to 1 with debt instruments, which include subprime mortgage loans. One of Alan Greenspan's comments after he left as chairman of the Federal Reserve was that he thought big financial companies would self-regulate in terms of risk. Big banks make their own rules about playing the game, and that allows them to win. However, they definitely don't understand risk as I define it.

There are other major factors that are probably too long-term to consider right now, but what about the long-term impact of global warming? Is the United States on the downside as an economic power? What happens when the U.S. dollar is dropped as the world's reserve currency? When you think about these factors and keep tabs on them, you are not surprised when the stock market suddenly crashes or major reversals suddenly occur in whatever you are doing. Thus, it is very important to develop a business plan (as a trader) that takes into account some of these factors. I publish a monthly diagram that to me illustrates what is going on in the world. It comes out around the first of the month in my free weekly e-mail, *Tharp's Thoughts*. Figure 2-1 shows the big picture as of November 21, 2008.

Today, the entire world economic picture can be represented by the relative strength of ETFs representing various aspects of the global economy. On November 21, the economy looked rather dismal. The top-performing areas are in green, average areas are in yellow, and the worst-performing areas are in brown.

The column on the far left represents the Asian equity markets and foreign currencies. We had a few good performers in the currencies: the Japanese yen and the U.S. dollar.

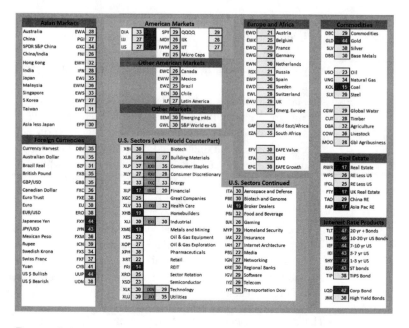

FIGURE 2-1. The Van Tharp Institute synopsis of the big picture in November 2008

The top center section represents the American economy. The major U.S. areas are in the top box. Other markets in the Americas appear below that. The bottom portion shows the major sectors of the U.S. economy with their global counterparts. Here you can see that the financial sector, the homebuilding sector, minerals and mining, and real estate investment trusts were all doing very poorly.

Europe and Africa are shown to the right of the United States. Nothing there was doing that well. Commodities, real estate, and interest rate products are shown on the far right. Gold and bonds were the top performers there.

None of the good performers showed a relative strength of even 50 (the scale goes to 100), and this indicates how bad the overall picture was and suggests that unless you are very skilled, you should have been in cash. The top ETFs on November 21 were all ultrashort ETFs.

Table 2-1 shows a long-term assessment of the market types for the U.S. stock market during 2008 (through November 21).

Market Condition	Date
Volatile Bear	11/21/08
Volatile Bear	11/14/08
Volatile Bear	11/07/08
Volatile Bear	10/31/08
Volatile Bear	10/24/08
Volatile Bear	10/17/08
Volatile Bear	10/10/08
Volatile Bear	10/03/08
Volatile Sideways	09/26/08
Volatile Sideways	09/19/08
Volatile Sideways	09/12/08
Volatile Bear	09/06/08
Volatile Bear	08/29/08
Volatile Bear	08/22/08
Volatile Bear	08/15/08
Volatile Bear	08/08/08
Volatile Bear	08/01/08
Volatile Bear	07/25/08
Volatile Bear	07/18/08
Volatile Bear	07/11/08
Volatile Sideways	07/04/08
Volatile Bear	06/27/08
Volatile Sideways	06/20/08
Volatile Sideways	06/13/08
Volatile Bull	06/06/08
Volatile Bull	05/31/08
Volatile Sideways	05/23/08
Volatile Sideways	05/16/08
Volatile Sideways	05/09/08
Volatile Bull	05/02/08
Volatile Sideways	04/25/08
Volatile Sideways	04/18/08
Volatile Sideways	04/11/08
Volatile Sideways	04/04/08
Volatile Bear	03/28/08
Volatile Bear	03/21/08
Volatile Bear	03/14/08
Volatile Bear	03/07/08
Volatile Bear	02/29/08
Volatile Bear	02/23/08
Volatile Bear	02/15/08
Volatile Bear	02/08/08
Volatile Sideways	02/01/08
Volatile Bear	01/26/08
Volatile Bear	01/18/08
Volatile Bear	01/11/08
Volatile Bear	01/04/08

TABLE 2-1 Market Type in 2008 (Based on Rolling 13-Week Windows)

Note that the entire year was classified as volatile and that most of the year was bearish. The weekly market types represent 13-week rolling windows. Note that 30 of them were bearish through November 21.

Do you think a regular look at the big picture in this manner would be useful? I certainly do. Doesn't it give you a better picture of how to trade in the current conditions?

What it tells you is obvious: You should have been either in cash or short. You probably could have had that position throughout 2008 (if you survived the period from April 2008 through June 2008).

It's important that you understand that my idea of the big picture could be entirely different from yours. For example, there are multiple ways to look at market types:

- I look at what the market is like each quarter (13-week period), but you might be a day trader.

- I measure volatility relative to what it's been over 50 years. You might be interested in volatility relative to the last 100 days.

Similarly, there are many ways to look at what is going on in the market:

- I look at the relative performance of the trading vehicles in the world with respect to what their ETFs are doing. You might think ETFs are risky and don't represent the world.

- I look at secular market trends that could last 20 years. You might not care about such long-term cycles. You simply may want the market to be volatile enough to trade today.

What's important is that you have a way to monitor what's going on so that you'll know when the big picture changes in the context of what's important for the way you trade; what's important, of course, depends on your beliefs.

What Are Your Tactical Trading Strategies?

Part 3 of this book discusses trading strategies in more detail, so I'm going to list only a few of the questions you should consider asking yourself here:

1. What are three noncorrelated strategies you can use that fit the big picture?

2. Do these three strategies cover the six major market types?

- Bear volatile
- Bear quiet
- Sideways volatile
- Sideways quiet
- Bull volatile
- Bull quiet

In other words, do you know how your system performs in each of these market types? Do you have all of them covered, or are there some markets that you'll avoid trading?

3. What setups do you use before entry?

4. What is your timing signal for entry?

5. What is your worst-case loss going to be, and how is it determined?

6. How will you take profits?

7. What is the expectancy of that methodology? How good is the system? How easily will it be with this system to use position sizing to achieve your goals?

You'll need to keep up with the current market type, making sure you have a system that will perform well. If you do not, your only alternative is to stay out of the current market type.

How Will You Achieve Your Objectives through Position Sizing?

Position sizing to meet your objectives is an important part of your trading business plan. You need to have specific objectives. You have to understand that your system doesn't achieve your objectives; your position sizing algorithm does that.

If you understand this concept, you are way ahead of many, if not most, professional traders: those who cannot practice position sizing. For example, most bank traders and even many company traders don't know how much money they are trading. How could they practice position sizing? Also, most portfolio managers must be fully invested, and so they can use only a weighted form of position sizing.

You, fortunately, do not have any of these limitations, so it is essential for you to understand this topic thoroughly. Read Part 4 of this book and then study *The Definitive Guide to Position Sizing.*[3]

---

[3]Van K. Tharp. *The Definitive Guide to Position Sizing.* Cary, NC: IITM, 2008.

Dealing with Your Challenges

Part 1 of this book involved assessing your strengths and challenges and developing a plan for dealing with them. You now need to summarize that material and include it in your business plan.

How prepared are you for a trading career? How did you do in the tests given earlier in this book? What is your trading personality? What are the strengths and challenges of that personality? What are your beliefs about yourself, especially the limiting ones?

Once you have all this material written down, you need to develop a plan for dealing with it. You should answer the following questions:

1. What do I need to do on a daily basis to keep myself disciplined and on track?

2. What are the major emotional issues that come up for me, and how will I deal with them?

3. What is my ongoing plan for working on myself so that self-sabotage is avoided?

4. How can I make myself more efficient as a trader?

5. How can I recognize problems as they come into my trading and deal with them before they become self-sabotage?

My suggestion here is to read through all the ideas in Part 1 about how to deal with these sorts of issues on an ongoing basis. Practice working with them and then develop a regular procedure that you can follow.

This area is very important and will give you a huge edge. Let me demonstrate how important that edge is with an example.

In January 2008 a large mutual fund hired me to give a one-day workshop for its traders/analysts. I was speaking in a room of about 30 people who were controlling about $50 billion. They wanted me to speak about two topics in which they needed coaching: position sizing and psychological management. Initially I talked about position sizing, but they were clearly handicapped because, as a mutual fund, they were required to be nearly 100% invested. They could not short, and they could not retreat to cash in bad times.

I explained how they could buy their benchmark and then overweight and underweight certain components as a form of position sizing. It was clear that they partially understood that concept. Their best performer in 2007 was someone who had an 8% weight in one particular stock throughout that year. It had had a stellar performance but was down more than 25% from its high, and he still had the 8% weighting in that stock. I don't know what happened to him, but the entire market they were trading went down another 50% by the end of 2008.

Then we moved on to the more interesting topic of psychological management. This was especially important since they had little control over their position sizing. I decided to show them an exercise to help them solve a problem, and the group picked its star performer to demonstrate the process. However, the star performer picked "being in front of the group" as his problem. This totally defeated the purpose of the demonstration. It was clear that the group was not interested in the topic of psychological management, as I was asked to end the talk early. They had decided that it was more important to spend the rest of the day analyzing the market.

I checked that fund toward the end of 2008, and their performance had been disastrous. Many funds would close the year with a similar performance. However, they couldn't do anything to practice good position sizing in such circumstances, and they didn't care about psychological management. I'm wondering how they feel about not taking that part of the talk seriously. Perhaps they were okay because their performance benchmark also had been disastrous.

Can you begin to see the huge edge you will have over many professionals if you take these topics seriously?

What Are Your Daily Procedures?

You need to develop a routine that will keep you performing at a top level. What's on the list will depend on you and what you need for peak performance. Here are a few things to think about:

DAILY TASKS
- ✓ TAKE A WALK AND MEDITATE
- ✓ REVIEW Y[E] TRADES
- ✓ LOO[K]
- HEALT[H]

WHAT ARE YOUR DAILY PROCEDURES?

- Do you need a pre-start-of-day self-assessment? What would that consist of? How will you do it?

- How will you make sure that you do what you need to do today?

- What will you do on a daily basis to prevent mistakes?

- What will you do on a daily basis to keep track of your trades and your thoughts about trading?

- What statistics will you monitor to keep track of your trading? Here are just a few of the things you can monitor if you choose to do so:

  - R-multiples
  - Expectancy
  - Standard deviation of R
  - Monthly return

- Daily profit and loss (mean and median)
- Annualized Sharpe ratio
- Ratio of largest winning day to largest losing day
- Volume of trading
- Number of winning and losing days
- Largest winning day
- Largest losing day
- Largest drawdown in dollars
- Largest drawdown in time
- Largest drawdown in percentage

■ What will you do on a daily basis to work on yourself?

- Diet
- Exercise
- Spiritual practices (e.g., meditation)
- Trading practices to keep you in top form

Spend some time thinking about these areas and develop checklists that you can use to monitor yourself.

What Is Your Education Plan?

How do you plan to improve yourself continually? Part of your plan should be continual improvement. Companies that invest in themselves and their employees tend to grow and prosper. How will you invest in yourself?

- What do you need to know to improve your trading in terms of both skills and knowledge?
- What do you need to improve about yourself to improve your performance?
- How will you get that information?
- How do you know your source is reliable? Remember that experts are not necessarily what they appear to be. The 2008 financial meltdown should convince you of that.

Make a list of everything you need and then develop a plan for ways to develop those skills and that knowledge. This should be a major part of your business plan.

WHAT IS YOUR EDUCATION PLAN?

Worst-Case Contingency Planning

The idea behind a worst-case contingency plan is to brainstorm what could happen. Approach the brainstorming as a creative exercise. If you do it from that perspective, there is nothing negative about it.

The purpose behind this planning is to prepare for what could go wrong. The market usually will find something that you are not prepared for and give you a great test of your fortitude. When this happens and you are not prepared, you become stressed and your brain shuts down. Typically, you respond in a very primitive way, but with a lot of energy. For example, you may scream loudly. However, this does you very little good and hurts your account.

Brainstorm everything that could go wrong. You might find that such problems fall into six broad categories:

1. **Personal Emergencies.** For example, one of my clients had a personal emergency and left a number of open positions to go deal with the emergency. When he returned, he came back to a financial emergency!

2. **Unexpected Market Disasters.** Examples include the 1987 crash; no one expected the S&P 500 to move 20% in one day, but it did. This category also might include events such as 9/11, when the stock market closed down for a substantial period. We actually had training for our Super Trader program that was like playing war games designed by someone who used to design games for one of the U.S. intelligence agencies. In that training, we had a scenario in which the World Trade Center was blown up. The reaction: "This is so unrealistic, nothing like this would ever happen." But it did, and within about five years after we'd done the exercise.

3. **Equipment and Data Problems.** What if something happens to your computer? What if something happens with your software, especially if you don't know it's happening? What if something happens to your data? What if you get faulty data and false signals? What if something happens to your phone or your Internet service? You need backups for all of these things. As the cartoon shows, what if your computer gets stolen?

SITUATION 53: NINJAS STEAL MY COMPUTER

4. **Major Life Changes.** These changes include having a baby, going through a divorce or a major breakup with a loved one, moving your office or your home, a personal or family illness, a personal or family death, and anything else that might be a major distraction, such as a lawsuit. These events tend to occur over a long period, and you need to plan how you'll respond to them. Sure, you can just stop trading, but perhaps there is another way if you work it out and practice it.

5. **Psychological/Discipline Problems.** This is where you plan for it and make sure it doesn't wipe you out.

6. **Broker Problems.** What kind of performance should you expect from your broker? What will you do when there are errors? Bad fills? A broker who questions your judgment? All these are items you should consider.

How to Make a Worst-Case Contingency Plan

Make a list of everything that could go wrong in each of these categories, plus anything else that might fit in a miscellaneous category. Plan on having at least 100 items or the list will be too short.

Once you've generated the list, come up with three ways to deal with each situation. If you have 100 items on the list, you need 300 solutions.

Determine which solution is the most effective for each problem and rehearse it thoroughly until it is second nature. This is the real value of worst-case contingency planning. The more you can rehearse globally, the less you'll have to deal with in a daily mental rehearsal.

Most people prefer to ignore this section of their plan, but it really is the most important.

Sometimes even good things can be a disaster. In my company business plan when the company was much smaller, I once considered that one of the worst things that could happen would be a large order that might take me several months to fill because I didn't have enough stock. People often don't think about how good news can be a disaster.

Mentally Rehearse Your Disaster Plan

Trading at a peak performance level requires that you know exactly how to react in any circumstances. What happens if you are holding 8,000 shares of IBM and it suddenly drops 13 points? What will you do? What if you are day-trading S&Ps with about five open contracts and suddenly get a call from the hospital and learn that your spouse has just been in an accident and is in serious condition? What will you do? What will you do if there is a major stock market crash? What if the Dow Jones Industrials move up 20% in one day and you are short? Will you know what to do in these circumstances?

The key to peak performance is to have a set of rules to guide your behavior and be able to withstand anything that might cause you to break those rules. You need to set those rules before you trade and rehearse your disaster plan as soon as you have one.

Normally, you have a conscious processing capacity of about seven chunks of information. However, under stress the body releases adrenaline into the bloodstream. Blood is diverted from the brain, which normally gets 50% of the oxygenated blood, to the major muscles of the body. You suddenly have more energy (i.e., to run away), but your thinking capacity is diminished. Typically, when under stress, you revert to primitive behavior, but with more energy. This is fine if you must run away from a predator, but it is disastrous if you have to think quickly about a market situation.

The trick to dealing with such a situation is to rehearse it in your mind before it happens. When you've done that, your unconscious mind will know exactly what to do and stress won't be a factor. You'll just do it.

I was introduced to the power of mental rehearsal by an NLP instructor who was a world-class cyclist. To maintain his world-class standing, he had to cycle about 100 miles a day on Southern California roads. About once every 5,000 miles something dangerous would happen. Several of those mishaps nearly cost him his life. As a result, he decided that if he was to live a normal life span, he had to give up cycling or take some sort of precaution. He chose the precaution: mental rehearsal.

He took his cycle to a field, sat on it, and for two hours thought through every scenario he could come up with that could be disastrous. For each potential disaster, he worked out a course of action and rehearsed it many times in his mind until it seemed like second nature.

Several months later he was doing his daily cycling, traveling at a high speed in heavy highway traffic. When he happened to look down at his front tire, he noticed that it had a bubble. Within seconds a major blowout was going to happen. Before he could even think about it, he did a flip over the handlebars. He landed on his feet with the cycle on his back. If he had not done that, the tire would have burst, probably within the next few seconds, and sent him flying into oncoming traffic.

When he stopped to think about what had happened, he realized that the flip was one of the behaviors he had rehearsed in the field that day. Mental rehearsal had saved his life. It could save your life too—at least your financial life.

Go through steps 1 through 3. Use your mind to make certain that you are ready for whatever the markets bring.

1. Before you start trading, make sure you have a plan to guide your trading. When do you exit to abort a trade? When will you take profits? What could distract you from your plan?

2. Once your plan is developed, brainstorm to determine everything that might go wrong with your plan or your life. This is not an opportunity to get morbid. Instead, consider it a creative challenge to prevent problems.

3. Develop a plan of action for everything that could go wrong. Mentally rehearse that plan until it becomes second nature.

Systems Other Than Trading Systems

Every business has many systems; by a system I mean something automatic that really helps people know what to do in running a business. For example, a fast-food restaurant will have systems to help the employees greet customers and serve them within a minute. It also will have systems for preparing food, cleaning up, managing cash flow, dealing with the problems that arise, and so on. Your trading business needs such systems too.

Cash Flow

The most important of those systems has to do with cash flow and budgeting. What is it going to cost to run your business? What does equipment cost every month? What does Internet connectivity cost every month? What do you pay for data? What do you pay for education? How about subscriptions? What else is part of your regular monthly outflow? How about research time and perhaps your salary?

All this should give you an idea of what you need to make every month to have a profitable business. What is your hourly wage as a trader? Are you making below minimum wage? What is your salary? All this should be answered (or at least well planned) in a very detailed manner in your business plan.

Customer Relationship System

When trading for others, you will need to get customers; you'll need some sort of marketing of your business. How will you legally let people know about what you can do for them? That should be a complete plan or at least a section of your business plan.

Next, you need to know how to keep your customers happy. How will you deal with customers who call on a regular basis with questions about your trading? That can be a real distraction. What will you do to minimize the need for your customers to call you? For example, you might want to have a newsletter go out to them weekly or monthly. How will you report results to them? How will you manage things when your results are poor?

Just as important, how will you manage things when you do well and your customers get excited and want that performance to continue?

DEALING WITH CUSTOMERS' CALLS ON A REGULAR BASIS?

Back Office Management

The next issue is your back office. How will you keep track of your customers? How will you send statements to them? How will you keep track of your performance, especially if you are managing a lot of individual accounts? How will you do bookkeeping? These are just a few of the questions you'll need to answer with respect to your back office. You need to plan for this.

Data Management

How will you manage your data? What if there are errors in the data? What if you have errors in your trade fulfillment?

How will you deal with data? Is your historical testing adequate for making decisions? For example, if you test

30 years of S&P 500 data, are you testing on today's S&P 500 or testing the S&P 500 data that actually existed for the years of your testing?

Does your data account for splits, dividends, and any other adjustments?

If you are trading currencies, do you have 24-hour data? For how far back? If you are trading futures, do you have continuous contracts?

What happens if there are errors in the data you are testing or, worse, errors in the data you are trading? What's your plan?

Doing Research

What beliefs do you have about conducting ongoing research? Look at the systems you are happy with and determine how well they will work in the six market conditions. Do you have something that will work well under each condition? If you do not, what's your plan for developing something, or are there certain conditions in which you just will go to cash?

Operations

How will you run the business? What equipment is necessary for your business? How will you make sure that everything works? Do you have other responsibilities, and if so, how will you coordinate them with your business operations? What will you do if anything critical goes wrong with any key aspect of the business? These are a few of the many questions that should be answered in the operations section of your business plan.

Organization and Management

What kind of organization will you elect to use for your business? Sole proprietor? Corporation? Limited partnership with a C corporation as a general partner? Will you elect trader status? How will it all work?

In addition, will you do it all yourself or have employees? It's difficult to become infinitely wealthy through trading if you are self-employed because you still have to work. However, if you can design a system that your employees can run for you, that's another story.

The Four Quadrants

I probably did 15 seminars with Tom Basso (who was featured in *The New Market Wizards* by Jack Schwager) in the early 1990s. We also talked endlessly over meals, and I interviewed Tom twice in my monthly newsletter. During that time, one statement that Tom repeated was "I'm a businessman first and a trader second." His businesslike approach was always the key to his success, and I'd like to explore that approach in detail in this section because the quadrant you operate on in business also will apply to the way you operate as a trader.

In the late 1990s, I also did several Infinite Wealth workshops with Robert Kiyosaki, and so I became very familiar with his thinking. In their book *The Cashflow Quadrant*,[4] Robert Kiyosaki and Sharon Lechter explore four types of people. These types are separated by their cash flow patterns. People on the left side of the quadrant—the employee and the self-employed person—work for money. People on the right side of the quadrant—the business owner and the investor—have money working for them. The four quadrants are fascinating because they also perfectly describe various types of traders. The most successful traders are going to be on the right side of the quadrant.

The Employee Trader *Works for* the System

If you work at a job (which just happens to be trading) and get paid a salary for doing it, you are an employee trader. Kiyosaki doesn't really define the word *system* in his book despite using it extensively. However, he gives many examples of systems. For example, the Marine Corps has a system that allows Marines to accomplish their objectives with a minimum loss of life. Soldiers either follow the system or die. Similarly, as I mentioned previously, McDonald's has many systems. Each franchise runs on hundreds of systems, and that is why McDonald's is successful. Employees follow the system or (1) the franchise folds or (2) the employees are fired.

---

[4]Robert T. Kiyosaki, and Sharon L. Lechter, *The Cashflow Quadrant: Rich Dad's Guide to Financial Freedom.* New York: Warner Books, 1998.

Thus, remember that employee traders work for systems; they don't necessarily understand the systems. I believe this is the key to why they are not necessarily good traders.

THE EMPLOYEE TRADER WORKS FOR THE SYSTEM

Bank traders, corporate traders, some mutual fund managers, and even people who have a job and just happen to trade on the side are good examples of employee traders. These people are motivated by security and good benefits. Thus, a top bank trader might make $50 million for the bank. However, she doesn't make that money; the bank makes the money. This trader simply takes a salary and probably gets a bonus for doing well.

Employee traders work at a job. They get paid with a salary, which is taxed before it is given to them. They work to get paid, which is their primary motivation. They would like to get paid more by doing better-quality work, but their primary thinking is that if I do X, I'll get paid. For them, the "security" of their salary and their "benefits" are more important than the "money."

I once considered working with the forex traders of a large New York bank. The treasurer gave me a good idea of what I was in for when he made the following statement: "I don't want any of our traders making over 20%. If they make over 20%, they could lose over 20%. Furthermore, they'd want huge bonuses, and then they'd be making more money than me." Even though this man was a key person in the bank, he was still an employee and had an employee mentality.

I've noticed that the worst traders I work with are typically employee traders. They know the least about trading, and they generally make very poor traders. Furthermore, people who have an employee mentality and a full-time job (i.e., they are into security and benefits) also make poor traders when they try to do it as a vocation. For example, most people consider stockbrokers to be traders. However, stockbrokers are really employees (to the extent that they receive a salary) who are paid to sell stocks. They are self-employed (see the next category) to the extent that they depend on commissions.

When employee traders approach trading, they usually bring the employee mentality into play. They want to be told what stocks to buy or what the market is going to do. They are used to being told what to do, and they abhor making mistakes. Bank trading rooms, for example, usually hold daily meetings in which the employees are told what they should be doing during the day. That's the employee mentality, and it doesn't fit into good trading.

The Self-Employed Trader *Is* the System

This type of trader is someone who has quit his or her job to be independent through trading. These traders do not like to have their income be dependent on others. Instead, they want to rely on their own hard work. They want to control the situation and do it on their own. Most of the traders I work with have this sort of mentality in regard to trading.

The self-employed trader is quite often a perfectionist. Everything has to be perfect—these traders will settle for nothing less. Thus, they need a perfect trading system and are always searching for something better. They are also likely to be into discretionary trading because a mechanical system cannot do it as well as they can.

Most self-employed traders are usually off searching for ultimate control, looking for a Holy Grail system that perfectly predicts market tops and bottoms. The results are usually very unsuccessful. When self-employed traders are taught principles such as expectancy, trading for large R-multiples, and position sizing, they have a chance to become very successful.

The successful ones usually realize that they have limited capital and thus start to manage other people's money. When one starts to do that, many other systems come into play besides the trading system. Self-employed traders usually insist on doing everything themselves and subsequently run into severe limitations of time, know-how, and frustration. The result is usually failure. Most people who attempt to be professional money managers approach it from the self-employed perspective.

Are you in one of these two quadrants? How about the people advising you? Are they in one of these two quadrants? Now let's look at the two quadrants on the right side.

The Business-Owner Trader
Owns and Develops the Systems

Let's look at the people who take the next step—they treat their trading business as a group of systems. They make those systems as automatic as possible and then train other people to run them. You cannot be a perfectionist and develop automatic systems. However, you can develop such systems and free yourself.

Let me give you two examples. The business-owner traders I have met are total systems traders. Everything is computerized. Data come in, computers process the data, and orders are sent for execution automatically. These traders constantly look for ways to make everything automatic. If a task is repetitive, they computerize it to eliminate the need for a human being. The result is that the business-owner trader can leave the business in the hands of someone else and do other things. These traders know the systems will work because they have developed them. The systems might not be perfect. They might not make huge returns, but they work consistently within the parameters for which they were designed. Furthermore, business-owner traders also have systems in place for getting new funds, dealing with clients, managing the back office, and doing research on ongoing systems. When an employee leaves, they can train someone else to run the system that was handled by that employee.

There are several steps to becoming a business-owner trader. The first step is to be able to develop or purchase all the systems needed to run the business. As an example, the business owner would know that position sizing is a key portion of a trading business and have a system to account for that. He or she also would have systems in place to manage the research, the data, the back office accounting, and the other people who are involved—all the things we've talked about in this part of the book.

Once their systems are in place, business-owner traders must find employees to run the systems. This requires good leadership skills. A businessperson will own the system and hire good people to run it. Thus, the business ends up generating money for the trader without requiring the trader's time. The business and its employees work for the trader.

The Investor Trader *Invests* in Systems

Traders become investors when they invest in systems that give them a good return on their capital without requiring additional work. For example, if you read Warren Buffett's criteria for investing in a business in my book *Trade Your Way to Financial Freedom*, you'll find that a key criterion for him is investing in businesses with good systems that produce a high rate of return on the owners' equity. Once such things are found, no additional work is required. The money just rolls in from the investment. The trader/investor has money working for him or her.

PART 3

Develop a Trading System That Fits Each Market Type You Plan to Trade

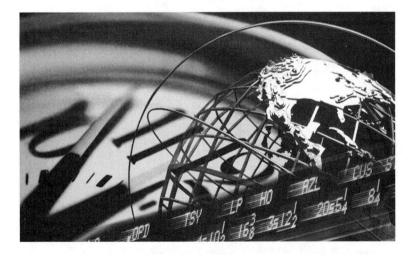

Designing a Trading System That Fits You

Jack Schwager's primary conclusion after writing the first two *Market Wizard* books is that all great traders develop systems that fit who they are. I tend to agree that this is one of the secrets to success. Here are some of the criteria you might want to think about in designing a system that fits you.

SYSTEMS, LIKE PANTS, SHOULD FIT YOU

1. You need to know who you are. How can you design something that fits you if you don't know who you are?

2. Once you know who you are, you can determine your objectives and design a system to fit those objectives.

3. What are your beliefs about the big picture, and to what extent must your system be able to fit those beliefs? For example, if you believe that the U.S. dollar is doomed to collapse over the next 5 to 10 years, how will that affect your thoughts about developing a trading system?

4. You can trade only your beliefs about the market, and so you need to understand what those beliefs are. What specifically do you believe about the market, and how does that give you an edge? When you understand these criteria, you can design a specific system with which you are comfortable.

Let's take a look at an example. Suppose you believe that markets are not really random because there are big trends that don't fit the price movements you'd expect in random markets. You perhaps believe that the best way to make money in the markets is to find and capitalize on those trends. If this was your primary belief, do you think you could do the following:

■ Buy things that are out of favor, things that nobody likes? Probably not because this doesn't fit the primary belief that you believe gives you an edge.

■ Sell high and buy low the way a band trader is likely to do? Probably not because that is a very different mentality.

I could give lots of examples of beliefs and lots of examples of things that might be hard for you to do because they don't fit those beliefs. I hope you've gotten the idea by now. You must determine what you believe about the markets that will give you an edge because you can trade something easily only if it fits your beliefs.

5. Next you must understand the various parts of a system and the beliefs that you have about each of those parts. For example, what do you believe about setups, entries, stops, profit taking, and position sizing? Again, you can comfortably trade only your beliefs. For example, suppose you want to catch trends but believe in tight stops. This means that you easily could get whipsawed in and out of trades a lot but that when you do catch a big trend, your total reward will be many times your initial risk.

6. One of my beliefs is that a trading system is characterized by the distribution of R-multiples that it generates. R refers to the initial risk in a trade, and R-multiples refer to the profits and losses expressed as a ratio of that initial risk.

We'll be discussing that in much more detail shortly. That distribution will have a mean and a standard deviation that will tell you a lot about how easy it will be to trade. Thus, you must decide what your system's R-multiple distribution must be like in order for you to be willing to trade it.

7. You also must also ask yourself, "What criteria must my system meet for me to be able to trade it comfortably?" Although I can give you lots of suggestions, this is still a matter of personal comfort and a big part of developing a system that fits you. Here are some sample criteria:

- Does the system fit my beliefs?

- Do I really understand how the system works?

- Do I understand how the system will perform under various market types?

- Do I trust my initial testing of the system?

- Do I feel good about trading it? Do I feel confident that I can trade it easily in my schedule without making any mistakes?

8. You also must ask yourself, "How can I use position sizing to meet my objectives, and what is the probability, given the system's R-multiple distribution, that I will be able to do that?" If you have an accurate sample of R-multiples, you probably can answer this question through simulations.

Finally, you must ask yourself what you will do to make sure your system fits all these criteria well enough for you to be comfortable trading it. If it doesn't meet some of your criteria that well, what will you do to make it fit? Or will you change your criteria?

Trading Concepts

There are many different types of traders, and one way to classify them is by the basic concept that they trade. Some concepts are diametrically opposed (e.g., trend following versus band trading), but you can trade any of them if you believe in it enough and practice low-risk ideas.

- **Trend Following.** The basic idea here is that you buy what's clearly going up and sell it when it stops going up. Similarly, you sell short what's clearly going down and buy it back when it stops going down. The key to doing this is to have a method by which you define when to enter and exit that gives you low-risk trades.

- **Fundamental Analysis.** The basic idea here is based on the supply-demand concept in economics. You need to analyze the market to find out where demand may exist and buy there (ideally, before it occurs). When you think the price is high enough that demand may drop off, you sell. You could assume that when the supply is low, demand will increase and start the market moving, but that isn't always the case. Let me give you an example in an area that I know well: rare U.S. stamps. Certain nineteenth-century stamps were issued in a very limited supply, and fewer than 100 are known to exist today. However, there isn't much demand for these stamps, and so the prices are pretty reasonable. However, if just 50 collectors were willing to spend $100,000 on very rare U.S. nineteenth-century stamps, the prices would go up 10-fold or more.

- **Value Trading.** You buy things that are way undervalued, assuming that one day the market will catch up with their value. There are probably thousands of ways to value stocks, and some are more useful than others. If you decide you like value trading, your job is to find one of the more useful methods.

■ **Band Trading.** Certain instruments (stocks, commodities, and currencies) trade in bands. You buy something when it touches, crosses, or gets close to the lower band and sell it when it does the same thing for the upper band. It doesn't matter which order you do this in. The key to band trading is to understand how to develop useful bands.

■ **Seasonal Tendencies.** Perhaps the real key to understanding seasonal tendencies is that what you find must have a fundamental basis for its existence. You can always use a computer to find meaningless correlations. For instance, say you buy XYZ in the last week in March because it went up for the next three days in 18 of the last 20 years. That could easily be a statistical fluke. What you are looking for is something like this: The stock market tends to go up between November and May because pension money tends to pour into the market during that period.

■ **Spreading.** This really gets into the realm of the professional traders who can create long and short positions with a lot of potential to move but with a much lower risk profile. For example, you can buy a December option and short the March option. You can buy one currency and short another. These are common practices among professionals who can do large trades very cheaply.

■ **Arbitrage (practiced primarily by professionals).** Here you find a loophole in the way things are done that gives you a huge edge. For example, before currency trading was available, one of my clients discovered that he could buy sugar in London in sterling and buy it in New York in dollars. He would spread the two markets to trade the dollar-sterling relationship, and he was the only one doing that. He said that in those days he'd have to unload one of his spreads if anyone wanted to trade sugar. Of course, this situation didn't last too long because people figured out what he was doing, but while it lasted, he said, it was like taking candy from a baby. The secret to arbitrage, of course, is to be able to find the loopholes and figure out how to capitalize on them.

■ **Intermarket Analysis.** Here we make the assumption that the price of one commodity (or product) is a function of what many other commodities are doing at the same time. It's not just a simple relationship among a few things. Thus, gold may be related to the price of oil, silver, the dollar, and a number of other currencies. These relationships change over time. Thus, the key to trading this concept is to evaluate a number of different inputs simultaneously to find the relationships that currently exist. Of course, this just lets you know the current relationship; you then have to use the key low-risk concepts common to all systems to make money from the relationship.

■ **There Is an Order to the Universe.** Here there are a number of subconcepts, including (1) waves of human emotion, (2) physical events that may influence human behavior, and (3) a mathematical order to the universe. All these concepts can be traded if they fit you and you use the appropriate low-risk techniques.

All these concepts describe the setups that one might have for entry. Setups are a small part of trading, but because people think that picking the right investment is so important, these types of concepts were developed. Trading styles actually are named after the setups.

Setups Are Not as Important as You Think

I noticed at the beginning of my career as a trading coach that when people talked about a trading system, they really were talking about the setup to a system. Setups are a very small part of what is necessary for a complete trading system, yet people still claim their setup conditions are their systems.

Let's look at one of the most famous systems around: William O'Neil's CANSLIM system. What is CANSLIM? It's an acronym for O'Neil's setups: *C*urrent quarterly earnings; *A*nnual earnings increases; *N*ew product, new management; *S*upply and demand; *L*eader or laggard; *I*nstitutional sponsorship; and *M*arket direction. When people talk about CANSLIM, they mostly discuss what each of the letters stands for in some detail. However, the CANSLIM setups, in my opinion, are the least important aspect of what makes that system successful or unsuccessful.

The following is a brief discussion of some of the setups you might want to consider:

1. *Failed Test Setups*. These setups occur when the market wants to test some area. For example, the Turtles used to trade 20-day breakouts, and so a 20-day high is considered a test area and its failure to continue is what might be called a failed test setup.

2. *Climax Reversal Setups*. Here the price goes parabolic to a new high and then falls. These setups are often the start of big moves in the opposite direction.

3. *Retracement Setups* (often used by trend followers). Here the market is identified as being in a clear trend (the first part of the setup), then it reverses (the second part of the setup), and then the trend continues.

4. *Time Setups*. This occurs when you think that some move is due at a particular period as a result of some "mysterious order to the universe" concept. If you have one of these, the time at which the setup is about to occur might be considered the setup.

5. *Price Data in Sequence Setups.* I gave an example of this in the description of the retracement setup above, but there are many different kinds.

6. *Fundamental Data Setups.* For example, an analyst may conclude that there is pent-up demand for a commodity. Demand usually means a potential to rise in price, and so the decision that demand is rising might be considered a setup.

7. *Volume Data Setups.* For example, the Arms Index, which involves volume data, might be considered a setup.

8. *Component Data Setups.* If you are trading an index such as the S&P 500, you could find important information that suggests a move by looking at what some of the individual stocks are doing. That's just one example of component data.

9. *Volatility Setups.* When volatility contracts extensively, it's often comparable to a spring waiting to uncoil and thus could be considered a setup.

10. *Business Fundamentals Setups.* Value investors have different ways to determine when a stock is undervalued, and that usually is a setup for them to buy. Warren Buffett has a number of business fundamentals that he reviews about each stock before he buys. These are all examples of what might be called business fundamental setups.

Entering the Market

Tom Basso and I were giving a systems workshop, but we were emphasizing the importance of psychology, exits, and position sizing. Someone in the workshop said, "I suppose you could make money with just a random entry." Tom said he hadn't thought about that, but he went home and tested his exits and his position sizing with a random entry system, and sure enough, it made money.

**PEOPLE ARE BRAINWASHED TO THINK THAT
SUCCESS IS PICKING THE RIGHT STOCK**

I was fascinated by the idea and decided to prove it for myself. I designed a system that traded 10 commodities over a 10-year period. It was always in the market on all 10 positions. When it exited, it needed to reenter long or short on the basis of a coin flip. My exit was three times the average true range of the last 20 days, and I risked 1% of my million-dollar account per position. It required a million-dollar account to always be in the market in 10 futures positions. I also added in $100 for slippage and commissions for each position, and so I had to overcome a huge amount of costs plus random entry.

With random entry, you are giving up any advantage that your particular edge has. The only way you can make money is to catch a strong trend occasionally and make sure that your losses are not too big and that you practice proper position sizing.

My results agreed with Tom Basso's: The method made money consistently. It didn't make a lot of money and you had to live through some nasty drawdowns, but over the 10 years it made money.

Why do people make a fuss about entry? I touched on this in talking about setups. People are brainwashed to think investment or trading success is all about picking the right stock. It's not!

Let me tell you about the first stock I bought when I was 16. I found the stock that had the highest per-share earning growth the prior year according to the 1961 review of the year by *Fortune* magazine. Thus, there was some research involved in my decision but no particular entry. Once I discovered it, I bought 100 shares for $800. That was my entry. I then watched it go up to $20 per share and then go back down again. Eventually it went to zero. My understanding is that a lot of people go through this sort of experience.

You could say that I bought the wrong stock. I could have bought Microsoft or Berkshire Hathaway in their infancy and made a fortune with my $800. However, for every stock like that, there are a thousand that eventually disappear, including many Fortune 500 companies. I basically ignored every important rule that I now teach people simply because I thought that to be successful you just had to pick the right stock. I could have had a 25% trailing stop. In that case, my initial risk would have been $200 (a 25% drop). When the stock reached $20, a 25% trailing stop would have had me sell at $15. I would have made $700 for a 3.5R profit. I didn't pick the wrong stock. I just didn't understand the rules for making money.

Let me repeat that statement: Success is not about picking the right stock. Of the original 30 Dow Jones Industrials, only one remained in 2009: General Electric. Most were dropped from the index, went bankrupt, or were absorbed by another company. That eventually happens to most companies. Picking the right stock and holding it until you die is *not* the magic formula for success unless you are very, very lucky.

However, today many, many people have this sort of bias. They are looking to pick the right stock and figure out how and when to buy it. For those of you with that interest, Chapter 9 of the second edition of *Trade Your Way to Financial Freedom* has everything you need to know about entry.

I discuss channel breakouts, moving averages, pattern recognition, prediction, volatility breakouts, oscillators, and more because so many different entry signals have been developed over the years. The key is to make sure you don't think it's the most important part of your trading, because it isn't. As we've already proved, you can make money trading with a random entry.

The Source of the Myth of Stock Selection

Since most people believe that stock selection is the key to making money, I'd like to share with you the source of that myth.

1. Mutual funds by charter are supposed to be fully invested. Furthermore, their job is *not* to make money but to outperform the market, which most of them cannot do. They cannot outperform the market because they generally invest in their benchmark index (e.g., the S&P 500) and charge you fees to manage your money.

LET PROFITS RUN

2. If you must be fully invested, you cannot really practice position sizing or proper risk control. Even asset allocation, which is actually position sizing, seems like an exercise in deciding which assets to invest in at any specific time.

3. Mutual funds, by the way, don't get paid for performance; they get paid by the amount of assets they manage. In other words, they get paid if they keep your money.

4. When the market goes up, most funds make money and most people are happy to be a little richer. The fund managers go on CNBC and talk about which stocks they like.

5. When the markets go down, most funds lose money.

6. Most people don't understand that the best traders get out of mutual funds and become hedge fund managers so that they can really trade. Very little of what they do involves stock selection. It has to do with cutting losses short, letting profits run, and practicing proper position sizing to meet their objectives.

Exits Are the Key to Making Money

As I mentioned earlier, I decided to prove to myself that one can make money with random entry. When you employ random entry, you are giving up any advantage that your particular setup and entry edge have. The only way you can make money is to catch a strong trend occasionally, make sure your losses are not too big, and practice proper position sizing.

How can your exits help you catch a strong trend? In a random entry system, when you exit, you'll enter back into a trade again and lose another $100 in slippage and commissions. Thus, you want your initial exit to be large enough to make sure that you don't exit very often. At the same time, you don't want to enter into a trend in the wrong direction, which would cause you to pile up huge losses. Thus, to make the random entry system work, I needed an initial stop that was big enough to keep me in the market while it was just making random noise movements or moving sideways. I chose to exit at three times the 20-day volatility or average true range.

I like to keep things simple, and so I made the abort exit and the profit-taking exit very similar. I trailed three times the 20-day average true range from the closing price. Thus, if the price moved in my favor, so did the trailing stop, and if the volatility shrank, the stop also would move in my favor. The stop was moved only in my favor, never against me.

As a result of this exit, I was able to stay in sideways markets a long time and not get stopped out. If I entered against a trend, I was stopped out quickly and hoped the random entry would reenter in the direction of the trend. Also, if I was lucky enough to enter in the direction of the trend, my stop kept me in the trend for a long time. It was that easy. With that simple exit, the random entry system was able to follow the golden rule of trading (cutting losses short and letting profits run) and thus make money overall.

The first kind of exit you need to know about is the abort exit. This is the exit that defines your initial risk, or what I've been calling 1R.

In reality, there are two kinds of initial exits: tight ones (1R is small) and wide ones (1R is big). Each has some distinct advantages. The wide exit keeps you in a trade for a long time and gives it a chance to start working for you. Thus, if you like to be right, you have more of a chance with a wide exit. Examples of this include the three times volatility exit mentioned above for the random entry system and a 25% retracement exit, which works fairly well for stocks. If you want to buy and hold stocks as long as you can, simply use a 25% trailing stop as an exit, adjusting it up whenever the stock makes a new high.

A TIGHT STOP WILL PRODUCE A SMALL R

The other type of initial exit is the narrow exit, which defines 1R as a very small amount. If you want to be right, you don't want this sort of exit because you'll be stopped out a lot. However, if you want large R-multiple gains, you'll find some advantage to tight initial exits.

Let's look at an example. Suppose you buy a $50 stock when it breaks out from a consolidation with power. If you put your stop below the consolidation, say, at $45, you'll probably be right a lot. However, if the stock goes up $10 in price, you will have made only twice your risk, or 2R.

Suppose you put your stop in at $49, a dollar away. If the move has power behind it, the stock should keep moving and you won't be stopped out. Furthermore, if the stock goes up $10, you've now made a 10R profit, or 10 times your initial risk.

In fact, you could be stopped out three times in a row, getting three 1R losses, and then make your 10R profit. You are right only 25% of the time, but your total profit is 7R.

At this point you might be thinking, "Yes, you make 7R, but you started out with a very small risk." That's where position sizing comes into play. What would happen if you risked 1% of your account on every trade? If you are up 7R, you'll be up about 7%, no matter how big or small R is for one unit.

Exiting a Trade beyond the Initial Stop

When you design an exit for your system, one of the key things to consider is the purpose behind that exit. You might have four possible purposes for an exit:

1. Produce a loss but reduce the initial risk

2. Maximize the profits

3. Keep you from giving back too much profit

4. Psychological reasons

Rather than cover each of these exits, I thought I'd focus on one particular goal and show you how to use exits to meet that goal. Let's say your goal is to follow a trend as long as it lasts. However, you want to have a wide initial stop so that you won't be whipsawed once you get into the market. You also want to give the position plenty of room to move. Finally, you want to capture as much of your profit as you can once you reach a 4R target. Note how these objectives fit a particular set of beliefs about the market. Your system always has to conform to your beliefs about the market or you won't be able to trade it.

To meet your initial goal, you need a wide stop. Let's say you pick three times the volatility of the last 20 days, as I described for my random entry system. That gives you plenty of room to make sure that the random noise of the market will not take you out of your position.

Second, you want to give your position plenty of room to move as it is going up. Again, all you have to do here is trail your three times volatility stop to meet this objective. Thus, every time you make a new high, your stop will move up to trail from that point.

Third, once you've reached 4R, you don't want to give much profit back. Thus, you decide that when your target is reached, you will shrink your stop from 3 times the volatility to 1.6 times the volatility. It's that simple. Your worst case at this point is that the market will retrace immediately and you will get stopped out. However, your new stop is probably only about 0.5R now, and so if you were stopped out immediately, you'd still have about a 3.5R profit. Of course, the market could continue to climb, and you are giving yourself a chance for a 10R profit or more.

SOME EXITS HELP MAXIMIZE YOUR PROFITS

All these stops are simple. I came up with them just by thinking about the types of stops that you might want to use to meet the stated objectives. No testing was involved, and so they are not overoptimized. No rocket science is involved. They are logical and make sense for meeting the objectives. They are simple. Note that you also have three different exits but that only one will be active at any one time: the one that is closest to the market price.

If you want to master exits for your trading system, you must learn the different types of exits available to you. Notice what each exit is designed to accomplish. Then, when you decide how your system is supposed to work, you'll find it easy to develop an exit that meets your goals.

Remember that your real goal in designing a trading system is to develop one that works well in one or two market types. That's pretty easy to do. The mistake most people make is to try to fit one system to multiple market types; you don't have to do that.

Start Thinking in Terms of Reward and Risk

One of the cardinal rules of good trading is always to have an exit point before you enter into a trade. This is your worst-case risk for the trade. It's the point at which you would say, "Something's wrong with this trade, and I need to get out to preserve my capital."

Most sophisticated traders have some sort of exit criteria that they like. However, if you are a novice and don't know how to do this, I recommend 75% of your entry price if you are an equity trader. That is, if you buy a stock at $40, get out if the stock drops to $30 or below. If you are a futures trader, calculate the average true range over the last 20 days and multiply that result by three. If the contract drops to that level, you must get out of the position.

Your initial stop defines your initial risk. In the example of our $40 stock, your initial risk is $10 per share, and I call this risk 1R, where R stands for risk. If you know your initial risk, you can express all your results in terms of your initial risk.

Say your initial risk is $10 per share. If you make a profit of $40 per share, you have a gain of 4R. If you have a loss of $15 per share, you have a 1.5R loss. Losses bigger than 1R could occur when you have a sudden big move against you.

Let's look at a few more cases. If the stock goes up to $110, what's your profit in terms of R? Your profit is $100 and your initial risk is $10, and so you've made a 10R profit. This is interesting because portfolio managers like to talk about 10-baggers. By a 10-bagger, they mean a stock that they bought at $10 per share that goes up to $100, in other words, a stock that goes up in value 10 times. However, I think a 10R gain is much more useful to think about and much easier to attain.

When our 1R loss was $10 per share, the stock had to go up by $100 to get a 10R gain. However, to fit the portfolio manager's definition of a 10-bagger, it would have had to go up 10 times the price you bought it for, rising from $40 per share to $400. What would that $360 gain be in terms of R-multiples when your initial risk was $10? That's right: It would be a 36R gain.

As an exercise, look at all your closed trades last year and express them as R-multiples. What was your initial risk? What were your total gain and total loss? What's the ratio of each profit or loss to the initial risk? If you didn't set your initial

Position	Profit or Loss	R-Multiple
1	$678	0.86R
2	$3,456	4.40R
3	($567)	–0.72R
4	$342	0.44R
5	$1,234	1.57R
6	$888	1.13R
7	($1,333)	–1.70R
8	($454)	–0.58R

TABLE 3-1   Expressing Profit/Loss as R-Multiples

risk for your trades last year, use your average loss as a rough estimate of your initial risk.

Let's look at how 10 trades might be expressed as ratios of the initial risk. Here we have three losses: $567, $1,333, and $454. The average loss is $785.67, and so we'll assume that this was the initial risk. (I hope you know the initial risk so that you won't have to use the average loss.) The ratios that we calculate are the R-multiples for the trading system. This information is shown in Table 3-1.

When you have a complete R-multiple distribution for your trading system, there are a lot of things you can do with it. You can calculate the mean R-multiple. The mean R-multiple, what I call expectancy, tells you what you can expect from your system on the average over many trades in terms of R.

"MEAN R IS THE EXPECTANCY"

Although I recommend that you have a minimum of 30 trades before you attempt to determine the characteristics of the R-multiples, we'll use the eight examples in the table. Here the mean R-multiple is 0.68R. What does this tell you?

The expectancy tells you that on the average you'll make 0.68R per trade. Thus, over 100 trades, you'll make about 68R.

The standard deviation tells you how much variability you can expect from your system's performance. In the sample our standard deviation was 1.86R. Typically, you can determine the quality of your system by the ratio of the expectancy to the standard deviation. In our small sample the ratio is 0.36, which is excellent. After 100 or so trades, I'd expect this ratio to be much smaller; however, if it remains above 0.25, we have an acceptable system.

One of Your Most Important Tasks: Keep Up with the R-Multiples of Your Trades

One of the easiest ways to keep track of the R-multiples in your trading system and its expectancy is to calculate them on a daily basis. Keep a daily spreadsheet with some simple information on it. You need only five basic columns:

1. An identifier column (what trade it was and when it was purchased)

2. Your entry risk (the difference between the entry price and the initial stop times the number of shares purchased)

3. How many shares

4. The total gain or loss when you sold the stock (yes, you can subtract commissions)

5. The R-multiple (column 4 divided by column 2)

You might want other columns, such as the entry price, whether you are long or short, the exit price, and the percent risk taken on the trade. However, these columns are not critical to obtain the R-multiples and the expectancy of your trades. We have sorted the R-multiples in Table 3-3.

When you do this kind of exercise, you gain important information. First, you are forced to write down and know your initial stop. There is no cheating when you do this; you must know the initial stop. This exercise alone will save you money. It will force you to have an initial stop and show you whether you are paying attention to it. If most of your losses are less than 1R, you are paying attention. If most of your losses are more than 1R, you are not paying attention to the stop or are trading instruments that are so volatile that you cannot possibly expect to get out at those stop levels.

The second thing this exercise forces you to do is define what 1R is in each trade in the simplest way possible. You're asking yourself, "What is my total, worst-case risk going into this trade?" and writing the answer down on paper. Again, this value is the entry price minus the stop price multiplied by the total number of shares purchased. Here 1R is confounded with the position sizing, but it also is in the profit and loss, and so position sizing cancels out.

Third, this exercise forces you to calculate the R-multiple for each trade. When you close out the trade, you compare it with the initial risk. Is it bigger or smaller than the initial risk, and by what magnitude? This information can be very valuable.

Fourth, this process forces you to start thinking about the ratio of reward to risk in each trade you make. You begin to learn that you should never take a trade unless the potential reward is at least three times as big as the potential risk you face.

Fifth, this exercise provides an easy way to calculate the expectancy of your system on an ongoing basis. You simply add up the R-multiples for all your trades and divide the total by the number of trades. The resulting value is the current expectancy of your system. By doing this exercise, you'll know where you stand every day. You'll know the expectancy of your system— how much you'll make per trade on average as a function of your initial risk—and know why it changes.

For example, when I asked one of my clients to send me a spreadsheet of his scalping trades, it became clear to me that his trading was not at all as he'd described it. Those trades are shown in Table 3-2. For example, he had characterized his system as a 60% system that risks a few cents per share on 1,000 shares to gain a few cents per share on those 1,000 shares, in other words, a 60% system with winners and losers that are both 1R. The fact that he didn't know the distribution of his R-multiples—as most traders don't—shows why this is such an important exercise. Although he was right about the system being correct 60% of the time, he was wrong about the R-multiples. Half his profit came from a single trade (trade 7). Although only 40 trades were given in the sample, I expected that this was typical of his trading.

Another interesting aspect of his trading was four consecutive losses, all of which were 1.5R or bigger. He also had six losses in eight trades. This is another nasty contingency that one may have to contend with while trading such a system even though the system has a reliability of 60%.

In addition, he had a number of losses that were 2R or more. I tend to suspect that many losses that big are psychological mistakes. Eliminating those mistakes is very important to doing well in trading.

Trade	Ticker	Strategy	Qty	Price	Initial Risk	Gain/Loss	R:Multiple	% Wins
1	XCIT	Short	400	44.375	100	550.00	5.50	1.000
2	XCIT	Short	400	40.688	100	125.00	1.25	1.000
3	XCIT	Short	400	40.188	100	400.00	4.00	1.000
4	XCIT	Short	400	40.375	100	200.00	2.00	1.000
5	XCIT	Short	400	34.500	100	275.00	2.75	1.000
6	XCIT	Long	500	35.500	125	**−156.25**	**−1.25**	0.833
7	XCIT	Short	500	28.500	125	1906.25	15.25	0.857
8	XCIT	Short	500	30.125	125	**−531.25**	**−4.25**	0.750
9	XCIT	Short	500	26.625	125	**−125.00**	**−1.00**	0.667
10	XCIT	Short	300	23.563	75	150.00	2.00	0.700
11	XCIT	Long	400	28.000	100	125.00	1.25	0.727
12	XCIT	Long	400	30.000	100	**−450.00**	**−4.50**	0.667
13	XCIT	Long	961	26.297	240.25	480.50	2.00	0.692
14	XCIT	Short	400	27.625	100	**−200.00**	**−2.00**	0.643
15	XCIT	Long	1000	27.813	250	**−62.50**	**−0.25**	0.600
16	XCIT	Long	300	41.906	75	**−121.88**	**−1.63**	0.563
17	XCIT	Short	500	40.625	125	31.25	0.25	0.588
18	XCIT	Short	500	42.000	125	**−31.25**	**−0.25**	0.556
19	XCIT	Short	300	37.563	75	0.00	0.00	0.526
20	XCIT	Short	500	38.496	125	**−60.55**	**−0.48**	0.500
21	XCIT	Short	300	35.125	75	9.38	0.13	0.524
22	XCIT	Short	300	34.000	75	412.50	5.50	0.545
23	XCIT	Short	300	33.250	75	**−93.75**	**−1.25**	0.522
24	XCIT	Long	300	37.875	75	**−37.50**	**−0.50**	0.500
25	XCIT	Long	400	29.188	100	175.00	1.75	0.520
26	XCIT	Long	400	28.313	100	200.00	2.00	0.538
27	XCIT	Long	400	29.484	100	**−193.75**	**−1.94**	0.519
28	XCIT	Long	400	31.188	100	**−200.00**	**−2.00**	0.500
29	XCIT	Short	100	35.063	25	**−37.50**	**−1.50**	0.483
30	XCIT	Long	400	33.813	100	**−200.00**	**−2.00**	0.467
31	XCIT	Long	400	33.000	100	75.00	0.75	0.484
32	XCIT	Short	500	34.063	125	125.00	1.00	0.500
33	XCIT	Long	500	35.625	125	125.00	1.00	0.515
34	XCIT	Short	500	35.125	125	156.25	1.25	0.529

TABLE 3-2   A Set of Scalping Trades

Trade	Ticker	Strategy	Qty	Price	Initial Risk	Gain/Loss	R:Multiple	% Wins
35	XCIT	Long	500	35.563	125	187.50	1.50	0.543
36	XCIT	Short	500	33.875	125	281.25	2.25	0.556
37	XCIT	Short	600	32.188	150	262.50	1.75	0.568
38	XCIT	Short	450	34.000	112.5	84.38	0.75	0.579
39	XCIT	Long	600	34.125	150	150.00	1.00	0.590
40	XCIT	Short	500	33.184	125	**−169.92**	**−1.36**	0.575
Expectancy						**3815.66**	**0.75**	
Total Profit/Loss								

TABLE 3-2   A Set of Scalping Trades *(Continued)*

R:Multiples Sorted
−4.50
−4.25
−2.00
−2.00
−2.00
−1.94
−1.63
−1.50
−1.36
−1.25
−1.25
−1.00
−0.50
−0.48
−0.25
−0.25
0.00
0.00
0.13
0.25
0.75

TABLE 3-3   R-Multiples Sorted

R:Multiples Sorted
0.75
1.00
1.00
1.00
1.25
1.25
1.25
1.50
1.75
1.75
2.00
2.00
2.00
2.00
2.25
2.75
4.00
5.50
5.50
15.25
0.75

TABLE 3-3   R-Multiples Sorted *(Continued)*

You can plug all of these R-multiples into a simulator such as the one that comes with my Secrets of the Masters Trading Game and start simulating what real trading would be like. Doing this can give you a lot of information about what it is like to trade this system.

Exercise

Make a table similar to Table 3-2. For each trade you make, put down your worst-case risk at the outside: How much would you lose if you were stopped out? This amount defines 1R for you.

When you sell the position, write down the total profit or loss for you. Divide this figure by 1R and you will have the R-multiple for the trade.

On an ongoing basis, sum your R-multiples and divide by the number of trades. This will give you an ongoing expectancy for your system. Notice how each trade affects it.

Overall, I would recommend that you collect 100 to 200 trades like this. At that point you will have a good idea about the expectancy of your system. In addition, you will have a fairly accurate picture of the distribution of R-multiples in your system, allowing you to simulate it. Remember to look at market type and take trades only for the market type for which your system is designed.

Six Keys to a Great Trading System

As they learn about trading, most people are exposed to a lot of misinformation. It's almost as if there were an intelligence agency putting out misinformation to make sure that the average person cannot trade profitably. Thus, it's very important for you to understand the six factors in great trading.

1. **Reliability.** What percentage of the time do you make money? Most people emphasize this. They want to be right on every trade because they were taught in school that 70% or less is failure. However, you can be right about 30% of the time and still make good money.

2. **The relative size of your profits compared with your losses.** We've already discussed thinking about your trades in terms of R-multiples. You want your losses to be 1R or less and your profits to be large multiples of R. This is essentially the golden rule of trading: Cut your losses short and let your profits run. It's one of the keys to success, but it is very hard for most people to do.

3. **The cost of your trading.** When I first started trading, it cost about $65 each time one got in and out of the market. Trading costs were atrocious. Now you can get in and out for as little as a penny per share. However, trading costs still can mount up in an active account. Several years ago I was trading very actively. I was up about 30% on the year and noticed that my trading costs totaled more than my profits. Thus, even with today's massive discounts, it still costs a lot to trade.

4. **Trading opportunity.** For example, if you can make an average profit of 1R per trade and you make 50 trades per year, you'll be up 50R. However, if you make 500 trades, you'll be up 500R.

5. **The size of your trading capital.** When your account is small, it's very difficult to make good returns, but when your account gets to a decent size, making good returns becomes much easier. Some accounts are just too small to trade. The reverse also occurs.

When your account is so big that you can move markets just by entering or exiting, it becomes much more difficult to make good returns.

6. Position sizing. Position sizing tells you "how much" throughout the course of a trade. It is probably responsible for 90% of your performance variability; that's how important it is.

Most people want to be right most of the time. However, you can be right 99% of the time and still be wiped out in any of the following scenarios:

1. You don't have enough money to trade, and the one time you are wrong you are wiped out.

2. Your position sizing is too big, and the one time you are wrong you are wiped out.

3. One loss is so big (regardless of position sizing) that it wipes out all your profits (perhaps you have small stops and your loss is a 100R loss).

Common Elements of Success

Most people don't realize that at any particular time four or five people may go long a position and another four or five may go short or unload a position. Each of them can have different systems and different ideas, and all of them can make money. They may have different ideas about the market, but they trade it because they've figured out that it is a low-risk idea. A low-risk idea is *an idea with a positive expectancy that's traded at a position sizing level that can survive the worst-case contingency in the short run and realize the long-term expectancy.* We might add that such ideas are low-risk ideas only if they are traded in the market type for which they were designed.

All traders can make profits—even with different concepts, different systems, and some taking the opposite sides of the same position—when they all use systems with 10 common characteristics.

1. They all have a tested, positive expectancy system that's proved to make money for the market type for which it was designed. We've been discussing how that's done.

2. They all have systems that fit them and their beliefs. They understand that they make money with their systems because the systems fit them.

3. They totally understand the concepts they are trading and how those concepts generate low-risk ideas.

4. They all understand that when they get into a trade, they must have some idea of when they are wrong and will bail out. This determines 1R for them, as we discussed previously.

5. They all evaluate the ratio of reward to risk in each trade they take. For mechanical traders, this is part of their system. For discretionary traders, this is part of their evaluation before they take the trade.

Can you begin to see how those five qualities will start to generate success? However, there are five more qualities that are just as important and in some cases even more important than the ones just listed. Before moving on, reread the prior sections and see if you can determine what they might be.

6. They all have a business plan to guide their trading. I've been talking about the importance of this plan for years. Most companies have a plan to raise money, but you need a plan to help you treat your trading like a business.

7. They all use position sizing. They have clear objectives written out, something that most traders/investors do not have. They also understand that position sizing is the key to meeting those objectives and have worked out a position sizing algorithm to meet those objectives. We'll discuss this later.

8. They all understand that performance is a function of personal psychology and spend a lot of time working on themselves. This area has been my key focus for many years: teaching traders to become efficient rather than inefficient decision makers.

9. They take total responsibility for the results they get. They don't blame someone else or something else. They don't justify their results. They don't feel guilty or ashamed about their results. They simply assume that they created them and that they can create better results by eliminating mistakes.

10. This leads to the tenth key quality: understanding that not following your system and business plan rules is a mistake. We've discovered that the average mistake can cost people as much as 4R. Furthermore, if you make even one mistake per month, you can turn a profitable system into a disaster. Thus, the key to becoming efficient is to eliminate such mistakes.

The "It Didn't Work" Mentality

One of the least productive things you can say in furthering your market research is, "It didn't work." I frequently give my clients research assignments, telling them a great area in which they can do research. I may see them again four months later and find out that they are working on something entirely different. When I ask about the research area to which I had directed them, the response is usually "It didn't work."

THE "IT DIDN'T WORK" MENTALITY

That response totally shuts off productive research as if there were no potential in the area at all. A much better response would be "It didn't work because. . . ." This sort of response indicates why it didn't work and perhaps even suggests an alternative course of action.

Let me give you a few examples of how this mentality has been used to shut down very productive areas of study.

One of my clients came up with what I thought was a very productive profit-taking exit. The exit started out with a wide stop and the stop stayed wide as long as the market was moving strongly. However, when the market started to level off or when the advance started to slow, the stop would get much tighter.

The net result was that one seldom gave back much profit. Doesn't that sound excellent? I thought so, especially since his system always gave a reentry signal if the market started to move again. However, about nine months later this trader was into a drawdown. I asked how his stop was doing, and he said he had abandoned it. When I asked why, his response was, "It didn't work when I added position sizing." There was no explanation why, which might have resulted in an alternative solution. Instead, the choice was simply to say, "It didn't work" and move on.

I had been working with another client in developing a good system. We had discussed high R-multiple trading, and he had informed me that he had a setup that could be used in the context about which I was talking. He reasoned that this setup would give him signals with profits about five times as big as he was risking. Furthermore, the signals made profits, he thought, about 40 to 50% of the time. I thought that the signal sounded great and suggested that he take only those signals for a while. In addition, he was to research the exact parameters of the signal and send me a daily e-mail. What happened? He never took a single signal. Instead, he stopped sending me e-mails and told me that the signal didn't work. I asked him to send me data showing me why it didn't work. His response was that he'd get to it one day but to leave him alone until he'd gotten around to it. "After all," he said, "I've already told you it didn't work."

Once again, a potentially great idea was killed by three little words: "It didn't work."

These are just two examples of dozens that I can think of, and every one of them illustrates an important point: The way you think about something can totally change your relationship with an idea. Edison was said to have had 10,000 failures before he invented a working lightbulb. He may have said "It didn't work" after any one of them, but those words didn't stop him. Instead, he determined why the method didn't work and used that information to find another good idea. At no time did he abandon the idea permanently by saying, "It didn't work!"

Know When It Doesn't Work

When you have a system or an idea, you must know when it truly doesn't work. This is the logical extension of giving up on a good idea because you think it doesn't work. When you've researched something well enough to know (1) you are not getting the performance you want and (2) the reason you are not getting that performance, you've taken an important step toward knowing that something doesn't work. Usually, the knowledge of why something doesn't work will give you important knowledge about what to pursue next.

For example, let's look at the idea of maximum adverse excursion (MAE), the idea that losing trades don't go too far against us. This gives you an idea for limiting your stops, but when you try to apply it to your trading, you may encounter some problems. Some profit increase does occur, but it may not be that significant for you compared with the complexity of the MAE addition. MAE doesn't work because (1) some losing trades exit at the MAE when they would have exited at much less of a loss if more room had been provided by a larger stop and (2) some big R-multiple winners are cut off and become losses. Since reentry isn't allowed, those big winners are never realized. These two reasons cancel the effect of increasing the potential R-multiple of those winning trades.

You might take this concept and decide that that's all you want to do with it. It didn't work, and you know why. That's fine.

However, you also can use the reasons for "failure" as logical stepping points for your next research idea. For example, I noticed that in the few cases in which big R-multiples are cut off, a reentry signal almost always will catch them. When you do trading research and determine why something didn't work, it will always give you a reason. This reason could point you to areas that could give you much more profitable results.

Trading Reality Check

Having modeled success in numerous areas—the trading process, the design of systems, understanding and using position sizing, and developing personal wealth—I'm amazed to see how we are almost hardwired to do all the wrong things. It's as if we were put on this planet to determine how many ways we can mess up our lives. How do you respond to a loss? Have you done simulations of your trading? Have you really worked on yourself and determined that it's all you? What decisions have you made about your trading and yourself?

Let's look at a simple example. Knowing what you know after reading this far, you should have many ideas for how to improve your trading. Is there not a good reason to spend a month (or six months) developing a good business plan and implementing many of these ideas? Of course not, so what is stopping you?

If you don't immediately feel the urge to carry out this task, it's time to do a little homework to recognize your self-defeating patterns and excuses. I'd like you to sit down and write several paragraphs on "The Story I'd Tell Myself If I Did Not Produce Meaningful Change in My Trading and Myself." Be honest with yourself. What are your typical excuses?

DO A REALITY CHECK ON YOUR TRADING

Here is one possible excuse: "I was desperate. I was
running out of money and needed to do something now. I really
didn't want to go back to work, so I had to make money now.
As a result, I really didn't have time to do a proper business
plan. Instead, I just made trades in the market."

You also have patterns of behavior, justifications for failure
or not doing something, rationalizations for how you are, and
so forth. So what is it? You might begin your rationalization
with "After going through Dr. Tharp's Super Trader book, I did
nothing toward creating meaningful change in my trading
because. . . ." Or your story might even be worse: "After buying
20 books to improve my trading, I have not looked at any of
them because. . . ."

You might get away with sabotaging yourself by not
making a plan or even not determining what you need to do.
However, for the 30 minutes it takes to do this exercise, give
yourself a break and be brutally honest with yourself. You know
that you'll con yourself in order not to make progress. Treat this
exercise as a test to determine exactly how you con yourself.
Can you be honest and tell it like it is, or is it more important to
justify the excuses and be a failure?

Go ahead. Take 30 to 60 minutes right now and start
writing your excuses.

What did you write? If you were honest with yourself, you
justified your limitations. You probably created a record that
includes many of the major thoughts and beliefs you use to
undermine virtually every endeavor you try. Furthermore, the
more honest you've been with yourself, the more valuable this
exercise will be for you.

What It Takes To Have Confidence

Here is an e-mail I received from a client:

> *Dear Dr. Van Tharp,*
> *Overconfidence presents a trading conundrum.*
> *I find I can't trade big or successfully without*
> *lots of confidence. But when I'm at my most*
> *confident, the point where I lose all anxiety,*
> *I tend to have my biggest losses. How can a*
> *trader retain a healthy level of anxiety while*
> *remaining confident enough to "stay big"?*
> *Sincerely,*

First, you have to know yourself. This isn't a small step.
Most people are not willing to go inside themselves and explore
because they are afraid of what they might find. Instead, they
just say, "I already know myself." But what if you have
unlimited potential and don't know how to tap into it because
you are not willing to explore how you are blocking yourself?

WHEN YOU PERFORM ALL THESE STEPS,
YOUR TRADING WILL FLOURISH

Once you know yourself, you can set up objectives that you are comfortable with and a trading system that really fits you. That's part of having the confidence to trade your system.

Let me ask you some questions, all of which are necessary to have a system that fits you:

- Have you written down your beliefs about the big picture, and does your trading system fit the big picture?

- Have you written down your beliefs about the market (what works and what doesn't), and does your system fit that?

- Have you written down your beliefs about each part of a trading system, and does your system fit that?

- Are your objectives clear, and do you have a position sizing algorithm that's designed to meet your objectives?

- Do you know what types of markets your system will work in and when it will fail?

Typically, if your trading system fits all those criteria, you'll feel really confident trading it. If it does not, there are more questions for you to answer:

- What are your criteria for feeling confident about a trading system?

- Do you understand how your system will perform in the six kinds of markets? (I'll address this later.) Here I don't mean just its average performance but the statistical outliers (i.e., two standard deviations away from the mean). Are you happy with that? Also, if your system is performing well above average, do you realize that and understand that below-average performance usually will follow?

- Do you have a worst-case contingency plan? Do you know how to keep most of those potential disasters from wiping you out? This is an important part of confidence. If you are not there, you shouldn't be trading.

▓ Last, do you have a daily procedure to keep you on track? These procedures are designed to (1) keep you disciplined and, more important, (2) prevent mistakes or at least prevent you from repeating mistakes. One such procedure is discussed in the last part of this book.

Trading is really a business. Most businesses fail because of lack of planning. Treat trading like a business, not a hobby. If you haven't done these things, you'll typically be the most confident at the end of a winning streak and then have your biggest losses, just as you said. If you have done these things, you'll understand the big picture for you and your performance will be much more consistent and elevated.

I've seen major trading entities that did not cover many of these points with their traders. Most of them performed poorly or eventually failed. Also, I've coached some entities (as well as many individuals) to encompass these points, and when they do that, they tend to flourish. What about you?

PART 4

Understanding the Importance of Position Sizing

System Quality and Position Sizing

What is the purpose of position sizing? Position sizing is the part of your system that you use to meet your objectives. You could have the world's best system (e.g., one that makes money 95% of the time and in which the average winner is twice the size of the average loser), but you still could go bankrupt if you risked 100% on one of the losing trades. This is a position sizing problem.

The purpose of a system is to make sure that you can achieve your objectives easily through position sizing. If you look at the ratio of the expectancy and the standard deviation of the R-multiple distribution that your system produces, you generally can tell how easy it will be to meet your objectives by using position sizing. Table 4-1 provides a rough guideline.

With a poor system, you may be able to meet your objectives, but the poorer the system, the harder your job will be. However, with a Holy Grail system, you'll find that it is easy to meet even extreme objectives.

Of course, there is one other important variable in your system: the number of trades it generates. A system with a ratio of 0.75 that generates one trade each year is not a Holy Grail system because it doesn't give you enough opportunities. However, a system with a ratio of 0.5 that generates 20 trades per month is a Holy Grail system, partly because it gives you more opportunities to make money.

Ratio of Expectancy to Standard Deviation of R	Quality of the System
0.16–0.19	Poor but tradable
0.20–0.24	Average
0.25–0.29	Good
0.30–0.50	Excellent
0.50–0.69	Superb
0.70 or better	Holy Grail

TABLE 4-1 Guideline to System Quality

I've developed a proprietary measure we call the System Quality Number (SQN™) that takes into account the number of trades. We've come up with a few important observations in doing research on this concept:

- **It's very difficult to come up with a system with a ratio of mean R to standard deviation of R as high as 0.7.** For example, if I take a system with a ratio of 0.4 and add a 30R winner to it, the net result is that the standard deviation of R goes up more than the mean does, and so the ratio declines. What you need for a Holy Grail System is a huge number of winners and a small variation in the amounts won and lost.

- **If you confine a system to a certain market type, then it isn't that hard to develop something that's in the Holy Grail range.** Keep in mind, though, that it is in the Holy Grail range only for that market type (e.g., quiet bull).

- **You need to understand how your system works in various market types and use it only in the types of markets for which it was designed.** This says a lot about developing systems and echoes what I said earlier. The common mistake most people make in designing systems is to try to find a system that works in all market conditions. That's insane. Instead, develop different systems that are close to the Holy Grail level for each market type.

I received a report from one person who was trading currencies from July 28 through October 12, 2008. Most people were losing huge amounts of money during that period. According to his calculations, the ratio between the expectancy of his system and its standard deviation was 1.5, double what I'm calling Holy Grail. Once he realized how good his system was, he started to position size at levels that are acceptable only with a Holy Grail System.

Table 4-2 shows the *unaudited* results he reported to me.

I've seen people making 1,000% per year before, but never anything quite like this. However, I'm willing to believe it is possible if he has found a system that provides a ratio of expectancy of R to standard deviation of R of 1.53, as is

Number of calendar days	107 (15.3 weeks)
Initial account equity	$13,688.14
Ending account equity	$2,234,472.78
Total margin level	<30% of account equity at risk (on average)
Leverage/lost size	100:1/standard lots ($100,000)
Total number of trades	103 (1.305 standard lots)
Total number of winning trades	91 (1,090 standard lots)
Total number of losing trades	12 (215 standard lots)
Average number of closed trades per week	6.7 (0.96 trades per trading day)
Total $ wins	$2,232,875.93
Total $ losses	$12,091.29
Net gain	$2,220,784.64 (1.70% earnings on $130,500,000 of currency controlled)
Winning trades, %	88.3% (target 40%)
Losing trades, %	11.7%
Average size of winning trades	12.0 standard lots
Average size of losing trades	17.9 standard lots
Average amount of winning trade	$24,537.10/trade $2,048.51/lot
Average amount of losing trade	$1,007.61/trade $56.24/lot

Average time in trade (calendar days) – weighted average of positions within individual closed trades and simple average of weighted average for each trade

Winners	3.66 days
Losers	9.89 days
Profit factor	184.7 (target: >3.0)
Reward-risk ratio (trade basis)	24.4 (target: >2.0)
Annualized ROI	55,344.1%
Largest consecutive winning streak	32
Largest consecutive losing streak	2
Expectancy/standard deviation ratio	1.53

TABLE 4-2   Results of Unaudited Holy Grail System

indicated by the data he sent me. However, his return was possible only because he then realized what he could do with position sizing with this system. His exposure per trade is huge and would bankrupt most traders.

Again, I have no way of knowing if the information sent me was correct. I don't audit trading accounts. My business is to coach traders. This e-mail was sent to me as a thank-you note for the insights he got from my advice.

QUIET BULL MARKET

Position Sizing Is More Important Than You Think

Most people think that the secret to great investing is to find great companies and hold on for a long time. The model investor for this, of course, is Warren Buffett. The model that mutual funds work on is buying and holding great investments, and the goal is simply to outperform some market index. If the market is down 40% and they are down only 39%, they have done well.

If you pay attention to the academic world, you learn that the most important topic for investors is asset allocation. There was a research study by G. Brinson and his colleagues in the *Financial Analysts Journal* in 1991[1] in which they reviewed the performance of 82 portfolio managers over a 10-year period and found that 91% of the performance variability of the managers was determined by asset allocation, which they defined as "how much the managers had in stocks, bonds, and cash." It wasn't entry or what stocks they owned; it was this mysterious variable that they called asset allocation, which was defined in terms of "how much."

I recently looked at a book on asset allocation by David Darst,[2] chief investment strategist for Morgan Stanley's Global Wealth Management Group. On the back cover there was a quote from Jim Cramer of CNBC: "Leave it to David Darst to use plain English so we can understand asset allocation, the single most important aspect of successful performance." Thus, you'd think the book would say a lot about position sizing, wouldn't you?

When I looked at the book, I asked myself these questions:

- Does he define asset allocation as position sizing?
- Does he explain (or even understand) why asset allocation is so important?
- Is position sizing (how much) even referenced in the book?

[1]Gary Brinson, Brian Singer, and Gilbert Beebower, "Determinants of Portfolio Performance: II. An Update," *Financial Analysts Journal* 47: 40–49, May–June 1991.
[2]David Darst, *Mastering the Art of Asset Allocation: Comprehensive Approaches to Managing Risk and Optimizing Returns.* New York: McGraw-Hill, 2007.

I discovered that there was no definition of asset allocation in the book, nor was there any explanation, related to the issue of how much, or why asset allocation is so important. Finally, topics such as position sizing, how much, and money management were not even referenced in the book. Instead, the book was a discussion of the various asset classes one could invest in, the potential returns and risks of each asset class, and the variables that could alter those factors. To me it proved that many top professionals don't understand the most important component of investment success: position sizing. I'm not picking on one book here. I can make the same comment about every book on the topic of asset allocation I've ever looked through.

Right now, most of the retirement funds in the world are tied up in mutual funds. Those funds are required to be 95% to 100% invested, even during horrendous down markets such as the ones in 2000–2002 and 2008–present. Those fund managers believe that the secret to success is asset allocation without understanding that the real secret is the "how much" aspect of asset allocation. This is why I expect that most mutual funds will cease to exist by the end of the secular bear market, when P/E ratios of the S&P 500 are well into the single-digit range.

Banks, which trade trillions of dollars of foreign currency on a regular basis, don't understand risk at all. Their traders cannot practice position sizing because they don't know how much money they are trading. Most of them don't even know how much money they could lose before they lost their jobs. Banks make money as market makers in foreign currencies, and they lose money because they allow or even expect their traders also to trade these markets. Rogue traders have cost banks about a billion dollars each year over the last decade, yet I doubt that they could exist if each trader had his or her own account.

I was surprised to hear Alan Greenspan[3] say that his biggest mistake as Federal Reserve chairman was to assume that big banks would police themselves in terms of risk. They don't understand risk and position sizing, yet they are all getting huge bailouts from the government.

By now, you are probably wondering how I know for sure that position sizing is so important.

---

[3] Alan Greenspan, *The Age of Turbulence: Adventures in a New World*. New York: Penguin, 2007.

Let me present a simple trading system. Twenty percent of the trades are 10R winners, and the rest of the trades are losers. Among the losing trades, 70% are 1R losers and the remaining 10% are 5R losers. Is this a good system? If you want a lot of winners, it certainly isn't because it has only 20% winners, but if you look at the average R for the system, it is 0.8R. That means that on average you'd make 0.8R per trade over many trades. Thus, when it's phrased in terms of expectancy, it's a winning system. Remember that this distribution represents the R-multiples of a trading system with an expectancy of 0.8R. It's not the market; it's the R-multiples of a trading system.

Let's say you made 80 trades with this system in a year. On average you'd end up making 64R, which is excellent. If you allowed R to represent 1% of your equity (which is one way to do position sizing), you'd be up about 64% at the end of the year.

As was described earlier in this book, I frequently play a marble game in my workshops with this R-multiple distribution to teach people about trading. The R-multiple distribution is represented by marbles in a bag. The marbles are drawn out one at a time and replaced. The audience is given $100,000 to play with, and they all get the same trades. Let's say we do 30 trades and they come out as shown in Table 4-3.

The bottom row is the total R-multiple distribution after each 10 trades. After the first 10 we were up +8R, and then we had 12 losers in a row and were down 14R after the next 10 trades. Finally, we had a good run on the last 10 trades, with

1 –1R	11 –5R	21 –1R
2 –1R	12 –1R	22 –1R
3 –1R	13 –1R	23 +10R
4 –5R	14 –1R	24 –1R
5 –1R	15 –1R	25 +10R
6 +10R	16 –1R	26 –1R
7 –1R	17 –1R	27 –1R
8 –1R	18 –1R	28 –5R
9 –1R	19 –1R	29 +10R
10 +10R	20 –1R	30 +10R
+8R Total	**–14R Total**	**+30R Total**

TABLE 4-3   R-Multiples Drawn in a 30-Trade Game

four winners, getting 30R for those 10 trades. Over the 30 trades we were up 24R. That number divided by 30 trades gives us a sample expectancy of 0.8R.

Our sample expectancy was the same as the expectancy of the marble bag. That doesn't happen often, but it does happen. About half the samples are above the expectancy, and another half are below the expectancy, as illustrated in Figure 4-1.

The figure represents 10,000 samples of 30 trades drawn randomly (with replacement) from our sample R-multiple distribution. Note that both the expectancy (defined by the average) and the median expectancy are 0.8R.

Let's say you are playing the game and your only job is to decide how much to risk on each trade or how to position size the game. How much money do you think you'd make or lose? Well, in a typical game like this, a third of the audience will go bankrupt (i.e., they won't survive the first five losers or the streak of 12 losses in a row), another third will lose money, and the last third typically will make a huge amount of money, sometimes over a million dollars. In an audience of approximately 100 people, except for the 33 or so who are at zero, there probably will be 67 different equity levels.

That shows the power of position sizing. Everyone in the audience got the same trades: those shown in the table. Thus, the only variable was how much they risked (i.e., their position sizing). Through that one variable we'll typically have final equities that range from zero to over a million dollars.

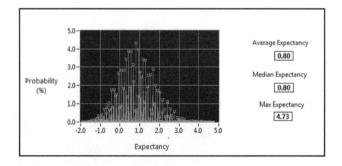

FIGURE 4-1. 10,000 samples from thirty random trades

That's how important position sizing is. I've played this game hundreds of times, getting similar results each time. Generally, unless there are a lot of bankruptcies, I get as many different equities at the end of the game as there are people in the room. Yet everyone gets the same trades.

Remember the academic study that said that 91% of the performance variation of 82 retirement portfolios was due to position sizing. Our results with the game show the same results. Everyone gets the same trades, and the only variable (besides psychology) is how much the players elect to risk on each trade.

If the topic is ever accepted by academia or mainstream finance, it probably will change both of those fields forever. It is that significant.

Three Components of Position Sizing

Performance variability produced by position sizing has three components (see Figure 4-2).[4] They are all intertwined, and so it is very difficult to separate them.

The first component is the **trader's objectives**. For example, someone who thinks, "I'm not going to embarrass myself by going bankrupt" will get far different results from those of someone who wants to win no matter what the potential costs may be. In fact, I've played marble games in which I've divided the audience into three groups, each with a different objective and a different "reward structure" to make sure they have that objective. Although there is clearly sizable variability in "within-group" ending equities, there is also a distinct, statistically significant difference between the groups with different objectives.

The second component, which clearly influences the first component, is a **person's psychology**. What beliefs are operating to create that person's reality? What emotions come up?

Three Components of Position Sizing

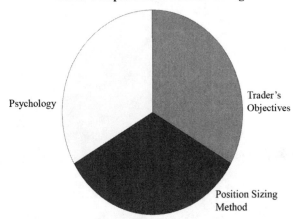

FIGURE 4-2. The three components of position sizing

---

[4]Much of the material in the rest of Part 4 was adapted from my book *The Definitive Guide to Position Sizing*.

What is the person's mental state? A person whose primary thought is not to embarrass herself by going bankrupt, for example, isn't going to go bankrupt even if her group is given incentives to do so. Furthermore, a person with no objectives and no position sizing guidelines will position size totally by emotions.

The third component is the **position sizing method**, whether it is "intuitive" or a specific algorithm. Each model has many possible varieties, including the method of calculating the equity, which we'll discuss later.

THE CPR Model for Position Sizing

A simple model for determining "how much?" involves risking a percentage of your equity on every trade. We've alluded to the importance of this decision throughout this book, but how exactly do you do that? You need to know three distinct variables.

■ **How much of your equity are you going to risk?** This is your total risk, but we will call it cash (or C) for short. Thus, we have the C in our CPR formula. For example, if you were going to risk 1% of your equity, C would be 1% of your equity. If you had a $50,000 account, C would be 1% of that, or $500.

POSITION SIZING IS CPR FOR TRADERS

■ **How many units do we buy (i.e., position sizing)?** I call this variable P for position sizing.

■ **How much you are going to risk per unit that you purchase?** We will call this variable R, which stands for risk. We've already talked about R in our discussion of expectancy. For example, if you are going to buy a $50 stock and risk $5 per share, your risk (R) is $5 per share.

Essentially, you can use the following formula to determine how much to buy:

$$P = C/R$$

Let's look at some examples so that you can understand how easy it is to apply this formula.

Example 1: You buy a $50 stock with a risk of $5 per share. You want to risk 2% of your $30,000 portfolio. How many shares should you buy?
Answer 1:   R = $5/share; C = 2% of $30,000, or $600. P = 600/5 = 120 shares. Thus, you would buy 120 shares of a $50 stock. Those shares would cost you $6,000, but your total risk would be only 10% of your cost (i.e., assuming you kept your $5 stop), or $600.

Example 2:   You are day trading a $30 stock and enter into a position with a 30-cent stop. You want to risk only a half percent of your $40,000 portfolio. How many shares should you buy?
Answer 2:   R = 30 cents/share. C = 0.005 × $40,000, or $200. P = 200/0.3 = 666.67 shares. Thus, you'd buy 666 shares that cost you $30 each. Your total investment would be $19,980, or nearly two-thirds of the value of your portfolio. However, your total risk would be only 30 cents per share, or $199.80 (assuming you kept your 30-cent stop).

Example 3:   You are trading soybeans with a stop of 20 cents. You are willing to risk $500 in this trade. What is your position size? A soybean contract is 5,000 bushels. Say soybeans are trading a $6.50. What size position should you put on?
Answer 3:   R = 20 cents × 5,000 bushels per contract = $1,000. C = $500. P = $500/$1,000, which is equal to 0.5. However, you cannot buy a half contact of soybeans. Thus, you would *not* be able to take this position. This was a trick question, but you need to know when your position has way too much risk.

Example 4:   You are trading a dollar–Swiss franc forex trade. The Swiss franc is at 1.4627, and you want to put in a stop at 1.4549. That means that if the bid reaches that level, you'll have a market order and be stopped out. You have $200,000 on deposit with the bank and are willing to risk 2%. How many contracts can you buy?

Answer 4:   Your R value is 0.0078, but a regular forex contract would be trading $100,000 worth, and so your stop would cost you $780. Your cash at risk (C) would be 2% of $200,000, or $4,000. Thus, your position size would be $4,000 divided by $780, or 5.128 contracts. You round down to the nearest whole contract level and purchase five contracts.

Position Sizing Basics

Until you know your system very well, I recommend that you risk about 1% of your equity. This means that 1R is converted to a position size that equals 1% of your equity. For example, if you have $100,000, you should risk $1,000 per trade. If the risk per share on trade 1 is $5, you'll buy 200 shares. If the risk per share on trade 2 is $25, you'll buy only 40 shares. Thus, the total risk of each position is now 1% of your account.

Let's see how that translates into successive trades in an account. On your first trade, with equity of $100,000, you would risk $1,000. Since it is a loser (as shown in Table 4-4), you'd now risk 1% of the balance, or $990. It's also a loser, and so you'd risk about 1% of what's left, or $980. Thus, you'd always be risking about 1% of your equity. Table 4-4 shows how that would work out with the sample of trades presented in Table 4-3.

Equity	Trade	1% Risk	R-Multiple	New Equity
100,000	1	1000	−1	99000
99000	2	990	−1	98010
98010	3	980.1	−1	97029.9
97029.9	4	970.299	−5	92178.41
92178.41	5	921.7841	−1	*91256.62*
91256.62	6	912.5662	10	**100382.3**
100382.3	7	1003.823	−1	99378.46
99378.46	8	993.7846	−1	98384.68
98384.68	9	983.8468	−1	*97400.83*
97400.83	10	974.01	10	**107140.9**
107140.9	11	1071.41	−5	101783.9
101783.9	12	1017.84	−1	100766

TABLE 4-4   Results of Risking 1% in the Game

Equity	Trade	1% Risk	R-Multiple	New Equity
100766	13	1007.66	−1	99758.37
99758.37	14	997.58	−1	98760.78
98760.78	15	987.61	−1	97773.18
97773.18	16	977.73	−1	96795.45
96795.45	17	967.95	−1	95827.49
95827.49	18	958.27	−1	94869.22
94869.22	19	948.69	−1	93920.52
93920.52	20	939.21	−1	92981.32
92981.32	21	929.81	−1	92051.51
92051.51	22	920.52	−1	*91130.99*
91130.99	23	911.31	10	100244.1
100244.1	24	1002.44	−1	99241.65
99241.65	25	992.42	10	**109165.8**
109165.8	26	1091.66	−1	108074.2
108074.2	27	1080.74	−1	106993.4
106993.4	28	1069.93	−5	*101643.7*
101643.7	29	1016.44	10	**111808.1**
111808.1	30	1118.08	10	**122988.9**

TABLE 4-4   Results of Risking 1% in the Game *(Continued)*

Remember that in this sample of trades you were up 24R at the end of the game. This suggests that you could be up about 24% at the end of the game. We're up 22.99%, so we almost made it. Equity peaks are shown in bold, and equity lows are shown in italics.

Because of the drawdowns that came early, you would survive. You have a low equity of about $91,130.99 after the long losing streak, but you are still in the game. At the end you would be up about 23%. Even though you risked 1% per trade and were up 24R at the end of the game, that doesn't mean you'd actually be up 24% at the end of the game. That would occur only if you'd risked 1% of your starting equity on each trade, which is a different position sizing algorithm.

You wouldn't win the game with this strategy because someone who does something incredibly risky, such as risking it all on the sixth trade, usually wins the game. The important point is that you'd survive and your drawdown wouldn't be excessive.

Types of Equity Models

All the models you'll learn about in this book relate to the amount of equity in your account. These models suddenly can become much more complicated when you realize that there are three methods of determining equity. Each method can have a different impact on your exposure in the market and your returns. These methods include the core equity method, the total equity method, and the reduced total equity method.

SO MANY WAYS TO CALCULATE EQUITY

The **core equity method** is simple. When you open a new position, you simply determine how much you would allocate to that position in accordance with your position sizing method. Thus, if you had four open positions, your core equity would be your starting equity minus the amount allocated for each of the open positions.

Let's assume you start with an account of $50,000 and allocate 10% per trade. You open a position with a $5,000 position sizing allocation, using one of the methods described later in the book. You now have a core equity of $45,000. You open another position with a $4,500 position sizing allocation, and so you have a core equity of $40,500. You open a third position with an allocation of $4,050, and so your core equity is now $36,450. Thus, you have a core equity position of $36,450 plus three open positions. **In other words, the core equity method subtracts the initial allocation of each position and then makes adjustments when you close that position out.** New positions always are allocated as a function of your current core equity.

I first learned about the term *core equity* from a trader who was famous for his use of the market's money. This trader would risk a minimum amount of his own money when he first started trading. However, when he had profits, he'd call that market's money and would be willing to risk a much larger proportion of his profits. This trader always used a core equity model in his position sizing.

The **total equity method** is also very simple. The value of your account equity is determined by the amount of cash in your account plus the value of any open positions. For example, suppose you have $40,000 in cash plus one open position with a value of $15,000, one open position worth $7,000, and a third open position that has a value of minus $2,000. **Your total equity is the sum of the value of your cash plus the value all your open positions.** Thus, your total equity is $60,000.

Tom Basso, who taught me methods for maintaining a constant risk and a constant volatility, always used the total equity model. It makes sense! If you want to keep your risk constant, you want to keep the risk a constant percentage of your total portfolio value.

The **reduced total equity method** is a combination of the first two methods. It is like the core equity method in that the exposure allocated when you open a position is subtracted from the starting equity. However, it is different in that you also add back in any profit or reduced risk that you will receive when you move a stop in your favor. Thus, **reduced total equity is equivalent to your core equity plus the profit of any open positions that are locked in with a stop or the reduction in risk that occurs when you raise your stop.**[5]

---

[5]This sometimes is called the reduced core equity method. However, that title doesn't make any sense to me, so I've renamed it.

Here's an example of reduced total equity. Suppose you have a $50,000 investment account. You open a position with a $5,000 position sizing allocation. Thus, your core equity (and reduced total equity) is now $45,000. Now suppose the underlying position moves up in value and you have a trailing stop. Soon you only have $3,000 in risk because of your new stop. As a result, your reduced total equity today is $50,000 minus your new risk exposure of $3,000, or $47,000.

The next day, the value drops by $1,000. Your reduced total equity is still $47,000 since the risk to which you are exposed if you get stopped out is still $47,000. It changes only when your stop changes to reduce your risk, lock in more profit, or close out a position.

The models briefly listed in the next section generally size positions in accordance with your equity. Thus, each model of calculating equity will lead to different position sizing calculations with each model.

Different Position Sizing Models

In most of my books, I talk about the percent risk position sizing model. It's easy to use, and most people can be safe trading at 1% risk.

However, in the *Definitive Guide to Position Sizing*[6], I list numerous position sizing methods, all of which can be used to achieve your objectives. My goal here is to list a few of the methods so that you can see how extensive your thinking about position sizing can be.

In the percent risk model, which we have described as CPR for traders and investors, you simply allocate your risk to be a percentage of your equity, depending on how you want to measure it. In some of the other methods, you use a different way to allocate how much to trade.

Here are some examples of ways you could allocate assets as a form of position sizing:

1. **Units per fixed amount of money:** buying 100 shares per $10,000 of equity or one contract per $10,000

2. **Equal units/equal leverage:** buying $100,000 worth of product (shares or values of the contract) per unit

3. **Percent margin:** using a percent of equity based on the margin on a contract rather than the risk

4. **Percent volatility:** using a percent of equity based on the volatility of the underlying asset rather than the risk as determined by R

5. **Group risk:** limiting the total risk per asset class.

6. **Portfolio heat:** limiting the total exposure of the portfolio regardless of the individual risk

7. **Long versus short positions:** allowing long and short positions to offset in terms of the allocated risk.

8. **Equity crossover model:** allocating only when the equity crosses over some threshold

9. **Asset allocation when investing in only one class of asset:** investing a certain percentage of one's assets, say, 10%, in some asset class

---

[6]Van Tharp. The Definitive Guide to Position Sizing: How to Evaluate Your System and Use Position Sizing to Meet Your Objectives. Cary, NC. IITM, 2008.

10. **Over- and underweighting one's benchmark:** buying the benchmark and considering an asset as being long when you overweight it and short when you underweight it

11. **Fixed-ratio position sizing:** a complex form of position sizing developed by Ryan Jones; requires a lengthy explanation

12. **Two-tier position sizing:** risking 1% until one's equity reaches a certain level and then risking another percentage at the second level

13. **Multiple-tier approach:** having more than two tiers.

14. **Scaling out:** scaling out of a position when certain criteria are met

15. **Scaling in:** adding to a position based on certain criteria

16. **Optimal f:** a form of position sizing designed to maximize gains and drawdowns

17. **Kelly criterion:** another form of position sizing maximization, but only when one has two probabilities

18. **Basso-Schwager asset allocation:** periodic reallocation to a set of noncorrelated advisors

19. **Market's money techniques (thousands of variations):** risking a certain percentage of one's starting equity and a different percentage of one's profits

20. **Using maximum drawdown to determine position sizing:** position sizing to make sure that you do not exceed a certain drawdown that would be too dangerous for your account.

Are you beginning to understand why position sizing is much more important and much more complex than you have conceived of in your trading plans to date?

The Purpose of Position Sizing

Remember that position sizing is the part of your trading system that helps you meet your objectives. Everyone probably has a different objective in trading, and there are probably an infinite number of ways to approach position sizing. Even the few people who have written about position sizing get this point wrong. They typically say that position sizing is designed to help you make as much money as you can without experiencing ruin. Actually, they are giving you a general statement about their objectives and thinking that that's what position sizing is.

Let's play our game again with the 0.8R expectancy. Say I give the following instructions to the people playing the game (100 people are playing): First, it costs $2 to play the game. Second, if after 30 trades your account is down from $100,000 to $50,000, it will cost you another $5. Third, if you go bankrupt, you will have to pay another $13, for a total loss of $20.

If at the end of 30 trades you have the most equity, you will win $200. Furthermore, the top five equities at the end of the game will split the amount of money collected from those who lose money.

Your job is to strategize about how you want to play the game. I recommend that you use the following procedure; it is also an excellent procedure to follow in real-life trading to develop a position sizing strategy to fit your objectives.

First, decide who you are. Possible answers might be (1) someone who is determined to win the game, (2) someone who wants to learn as much as possible from playing the game, (3) a speculator, or (4) a very conservative person who doesn't want to lose money.

The next step is to decide on your objectives. In light of the various payoff scenarios, here are possible objectives:

1. Win the game at all costs, including going bankrupt (the person winning the game usually has this as the objective).

2. Try to win the game but make sure I don't lose more than $2.

3. Try to win the game but make sure I don't lose more than $7.

4. Be in the top five and don't lose more than $7.

5. Be in the top five and don't lose more than $2.

6. Be in the top five at all costs.

7. Do as well as I can without losing $7.

8. Do as well as I can without losing $2.

9. Do as well as I can without going bankrupt.

Note that even the few rules I gave for payoffs translate into nine different objectives that one might have. Creative people might come up with even more. You then need to develop a position sizing strategy to meet your objectives.

The last step is to decide when to change the rules. At the end of every 10 trades, I assess the room to determine who has the highest equity. If at the end of 10 trades you are not one of the top five people, you might want to change your strategy.

Notice how this changes what could happen in the game. Chances are that I'll still have as many as 100 distinct equities, but chances are also that there will be a strong correlation between the objectives people select and their final equity. Those who want to win the game probably will have huge equity swings ranging from $1 million or more to bankruptcy.

However, those who want to do as well as they can without going bankrupt probably will trade quite conservatively and have their final equities distributed within a narrow range. The game makes it clear that the purpose of position sizing is to meet your objectives. As I said earlier, few people understand this concept.

One Way to Use Position Sizing to Meet Your Objectives: Simulation

One way to use position sizing to meet your objectives is to use a simulator. We will assume that there is only one position sizing method: the percentage of your equity you are willing to risk per trade.

Here is how we can set up a trading simulator by using the system that was described earlier. Its expectancy is 0.8R, and it has only 20% winners.

We know the expectancy will allow us to make 40R over 50 trades on the average. Our objective is to make 100% over 50 trades without having a drawdown of more than 35%. Let's see how we can do that with an R-multiple simulator. Figure 4-3 shows a position sizing optimizer.

I've set the optimizer up to run 10,000 simulations of 50 trades for our system. It will start risking 0.1% for 50 trades 10,000 times, then it will move up to 0.2%, then to 0.3%, and so on, in 0.1% increments until it reaches 19% risk per trade.

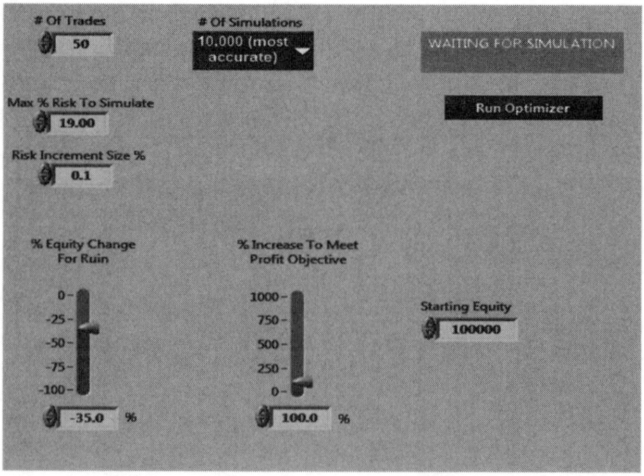

FIGURE 4-3. Using a position-sizing optimizer

We have a 5R loss, and so a 20% risk automatically results in bankruptcy when that is hit. Thus, we are stopping at a 19% risk per position.

The simulator will run 10,000 fifty-trade simulations at each risk level unless it reaches our criteria of ruin (i.e., down 35%), in which case it will say that was ruin and move on to the next one in the sequence of 10,000 simulations. That's a lot of computing to be done, but today's computers can handle it easily.

The results of this simulation are shown Table 4-5.

The top row gives the risk percentage that delivers the highest mean ending equity. Typically, this is the largest risk amount simulated because there will be a few samples that may have many, many 10R winners. That run would produce a huge number and boost the average result even if most runs resulted in a drop of 35% or more. Note that at 19% risk, the average gain is 1,070%. However, we have only a 1.1% chance of making 100% and a 98.7% chance of ruin. This is why going for the highest possible returns, as some people suggest, is suicidal with a system that is at best average.

The median ending equity is probably a better goal. This gives an average gain of 175% and a median gain of 80.3%. You have a 46.3% chance of meeting your goal and a 27.5% chance of ruin.

What if your objective is to have the largest percent chance of reaching the goal of making 100%? This is shown in the Opt. Retire row. It says that if we risk 2.9%, we have a 46.6% chance of reaching our goal. However, our median gain actually drops to 77.9% because we now have a 31% chance of ruin.

Optimizer Approach	Prob. of Objective (%)	Prob. of Run (%)	Avg Gain %	Med Gain %	Risk %
Max Return	1.1	98.7	10.7E+3	−72.4E+0	19.0
Med Return	46.3	27.5	175.0E+0	80.3E+0	2.7
Opt Retire	46.6	31.0	193.4E+0	77.9E+0	2.9
<1% Run	10.5	0.8	43.2E+0	37.0E+0	0.9
>0% Run	1.1	0.0	27.1E+0	24.6E+0	0.6
Retire-Run	37.9	11.1	93.8E+0	64.0E+0	1.7

TABLE 4-5   Position Sizing Optimizer Results

What if our objective is just under a 1% chance of ruin (being down 35%)? The simulator now suggests that we should risk 0.9% per trade. This gives us a 10.5% chance of reaching our goal but only a 0.8% chance of ruin.

You could have your objective be just above a 0% chance of ruin. Here the simulator says you could risk 0.6%. The risk is just above 0%, but the probability of reaching your objective of making 100% is now down to 1.7%.

Finally, you might want to use the risk percentage that gives you the largest probability difference between making 100% and losing 35%. That turns out to be risking 1.7%. Here we have a 37.9% chance of reaching our objective and only an 11.1% chance of ruin. That's a difference of 26.8%. At the other risk levels given it was 15% or less.

Just by using two different numbers—a goal of 100% and a ruin level of 35%—I came up with five legitimate position sizing strategies that just used a percent risk position sizing model.

I could set the goal to be anything from up 1% to up 1,000% or more. I could set the ruin level from anything from being down 1% to being down 100%. How many different objectives could you have? The answer is probably as many as there are traders/investors. How many different position sizing strategies might there be to meet those objectives? The answer is a huge, huge number.

We used only one position sizing strategy: percent risk. There are many different position sizing models and many different varieties of each model.

The Problems of the R-Multiple Simulator

Obviously, there are some huge advantages to simulating your system's R-multiple distribution to help you learn about that system easily. However, there are also some serious problems with R-multiples. Unfortunately, nothing in the trading world is perfect. The problems, in my opinion, are as follows:

- R-multiples measure performance on the basis of single trades but won't tell you what to expect when you have multiple trades on simultaneously.

- R-multiples do not capture many of the temporal dependencies (correlations) among the markets (in fact, only the start date and stop date of a trade are extracted). Thus, you cannot see drawdowns that occur while a trade is still on and you are not stopped out (i.e., by 1R).

- As with all simulations, R-multiple simulations are only as good as your sample distribution is accurate. You may have a good sample of your system's performance, but you never will have the "true" population. You may not have seen your worst loss or your best gain.

- R-multiples are a superb way to compare systems when the initial risk is similar. However, they present some problems when one or more of the systems have a position sizing built into the strategy, such as scale in and scale out models. In fact, in these conditions, you would have trouble determining the absolute performance of two different systems. As an example, compare two systems. The first system opens the whole position at the initial entry point. The second system opens only half the position at the initial entry point and the other half after the market moves in favor of the system by one volatility. If one gets an excellent trade (say, a 20R move), the R-multiple of system 1 will be better (bigger) than that of system 2 (larger profit and smaller total initial risk). However, if we get a bad trade that goes immediately against us and hits the initial exit stop, the R-multiple is *the same* for both systems, namely, −1. The fact that system 2 loses only half of the money system 1 loses is completely missed.

■ The impact of position sizing techniques (like pyramids) that change the total initial risk of a trade are difficult to test with the concept of R-multiples, since the R-multiple distributions of the trading systems (with and without the position sizing technique) cannot be compared directly. One way to evaluate the money management technique is to divide the trading system into subsystems so that the subsystems are defined by the entry points and evaluate each subsystem separately. For instance, each pyramid could be treated as a subsystem.

■ Since R-multiples capture only a few of the temporal dependencies between markets, simulations using R-multiples must be based on the assumption that the R-multiples are statistically independent, which is not the case in reality. However, one can cluster trades according to their start date or stop date and thus try to introduce a time aspect into simulations. When you do this, the volatility and the drawdowns become considerably larger when the R-multiples are blocked. In other words, simulations based on one trade at a time clearly produce results that are too optimistic (1) when you are trying to determine the performance of systems that generate multiple trades at the same time and (2) when you are trading multiple systems simultaneously.

Getting Around the Problems of Simulation

To get around the problems with a simulator, I developed the System Quality Number™ (SQN™). Generally, the higher the SQN, the more liberties you can take with position sizing to meet your objectives. In other words, the higher the SQN is, the easier it is to meet your objectives. For example, I commented earlier on a trader who claimed to have a 1.5 ratio between expectancy and the standard deviation of R in a currency trading system that generated nearly one trade each day.

Although I don't know if it is possible to develop such an incredible system, if he does have one, I have no doubt about his results: turning $1,300 into $2 million in a little over four months during a period when most of the world was having a terrible economic crisis.

In *The Definitive Guide to Position Sizing* I was able to show how, with 31 different position sizing models (93 total since each can use any of the three equity models), it was possible to achieve your objectives easily from the SQN. There are still precautions you must take because of the following:

1. You never know if your R-multiple distribution is accurate.

2. You never know exactly when the market type will change, which usually changes the SQN.

3. You have to account for multiple correlated trades. I did this with the SQN by assuming that the maximum risk was for the entire portfolio rather than for a single position.

Thus, in our example, with an average (at best) system and a ratio of the mean to the standard deviation of about 0.16, our best risk percentage was 1.7%. However, if we were to trade five positions at the same time, our risk per position probably would have to be reduced to about 0.35%. However, a Holy Grail system might allow us to risk 5% or more per position.

PART 5

More Ideas for Producing Optimal Trading Performance

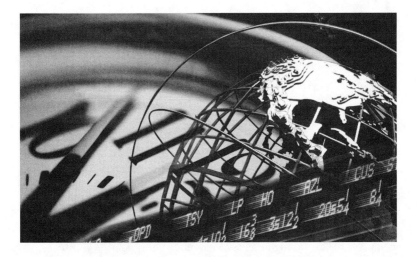

Keep It Simple

This applies to many things in life, including anything you might do in trading or investing: Keep things simple. The more you try to make things complex, the harder it will be for you to be successful. Keeping things simple works both in life and in the markets.

Your mind has a conscious capacity of only about seven chunks of information. You cannot hold any more than that in your consciousness. Have someone give you a series of 10 two-digit numbers and you'll probably find that you have trouble remembering more than five of them because of this limitation in capacity. If you attempt to do complex things with the market that require you to use more capacity than you have, you'll probably fail.

KISS (KEEP IT SIMPLE, SAM)

Keeping it simple doesn't mean that you can't use a computer to sort through the vast amount of information available about the market. On the contrary, I highly recommend it. However, it means that your methodology and your daily tasks do not have to be rocket science. In fact, the more you try to do, the less likely you are to succeed.

I did a psychological profile of a broker-trader who ranked in the bottom 1% of all the investors who had taken my psychological test. He had high stress, a lot of internal conflict, poor organization, no system, a negative attitude, and probably everything else you could name. I then did a 10-minute consultation with him, but he really needed several days. The key issue for him was how overwhelmed he felt by everything that came across his desk. How could he find good stocks when there were so many stocks? How could he follow any plan when his clients all had conflicting goals and motivations? His life was a mess.

This broker needed to do a lot of psychological work. His life was in chaos because his mind was in a state of chaos. Simplify the chaos in your mind and you'll simplify the chaos in your life. You can start doing that by deciding what you want in life (i.e., your dream life) and then focusing on only one or two simple goals from that dream life.

Second, he needed a simple system to track his own trading, preferably a long-term system that gave him only a few signals each week and required only that he look at the market after the close. That way, his personal decisions had to be made only once each day, away from the chaos of the market. That system could be something as simple as buying on a 110-day channel breakout, using the weekly volatility as a worst-case exit, trailing it from the close as a profit-taking stop, and not risking more than 1% of his equity on any trade. In his case, he needed to do a survey of all his beliefs about himself and that market. From that survey, he could begin to design a trading method that fit him.

These are all simple steps. Success comes from following simple steps. When you understand that and practice it, your performance will improve dramatically.

Understanding the Holy Grail of Trading

Let's look at judgmental heuristics. As I've mentioned, we have a
limited capacity for processing information. In fact, consciously
we can hold seven (plus or minus two) chunks of information.
That numbers is reduced dramatically under stress, when blood
flow is diverted from the brain to the major muscles of the body
to deal with approaching danger. In today's world, the danger is
usually mental and being able to run faster doesn't help us deal
with trading dangers.

UNDERSTANDING THE HOLY GRAIL OF TRADING

Every year the total amount of information we have to deal
with as traders doubles, but our capacity stays the same. As a
result, we've developed a number of shortcuts (i.e., heuristics)

to process information. In fact, psychologists have been documenting many of them over the years and have been calling them judgmental heuristics.

The overall conclusion is that human beings are very inefficient at processing information. In fact, some economists have begun to move away from the efficient market camp into the idea that markets are inefficient. They are inefficient because humans are inefficient decision makers.

This conclusion is excellent, but what they've done with it is not. What's happened is that a new school of economics—behavioral finance—has sprung up. Now economists are asking, "If markets are not efficient because humans are inefficient, how can we use what we now know about human inefficiencies to predict what the markets will do?" In my opinion, this is lunacy.

You might call what I do applied behavioral finance, and I take a different approach. I say that if most human beings are inefficient in the way they process information, what would happen if you started to make them efficient? Let's say a human being is 5% efficient in dealing with market information, although this is probably a high estimate for most people. What would happen if I could make a person 25% efficient? What would happen if I could make that person 50% efficient or even 100% efficient?

The results might surprise you. I previously talked about how trading systems may be considered a distribution of R-multiples with a mean (i.e., expectancy) and standard deviation that characterize the distribution.

Let's return to our system that gives you an expectancy of 0.8R and generates 100 trades each year. That system is not unrealistic. In fact, our sample system was barely a tradable system. I've seen much better systems. Yet that system, on average, will generate a return of 80R per year.

If you were to risk 1% per trade, you probably could make 100% per year trading it (i.e., 1% gets bigger as your equity grows, which is why you could make 100% instead of 80%).

However, because of behavioral inefficiencies, most people will make lots of mistakes. What's a mistake worth? I don't know for sure. We need to collect a lot of data to figure that out, and it'll be different for everyone. However, for now, let's say a mistake is worth on average 4R.

If that's the case and you made one mistake a week, you'd have 208R worth of mistakes, and you'd lose money trading a system that potentially could give you 100%. In contrast, let's say you make only one mistake a month (most profitable traders probably do that). If you make a mistake a month, that's 48R lost out of 80R, leaving you 32R in profits. During a severe drawdown in the system, you might give up on the system, thinking it no longer works.

Let's look at the trader who makes one mistake a month. Our system generates about seven to eight trades per month, and so we could say that she makes one mistake per eight trades in executing the system; in other words, she's 87.5% efficient. However, in terms of profits, she's made only 32R out of a potential 80R, and so it looks like she's only 40% efficient.

What would happen if she could become 60% efficient, or 80%, or more? The increase in return would be phenomenal. Perhaps it's time to read about some of the common inefficiencies that human beings have and learn how to become more efficient as a trader. Follow the suggestions in this book and you'll become much more efficient.

Miscellaneous Ways to Make Money in a Trading Business

You can grow your business, especially when capital isn't the problem. Instead, your problem is finding the best use for your capital. When you think about these methods, they may seem obvious, but most people don't think about them enough. Here are the key ways you can grow your business:

1. **First, develop new, improved trading systems.** Each system, especially if it is not correlated with the other systems, can help you make more profits. Continue to do research to find new systems that can become new profit centers for your trading research. By the way, some of your systems may stop working in certain market conditions, and so it's always good to have more systems in the pipeline.

2. **Second, find more markets in which to apply each system.** Let's say you develop a great system that works on the S&P 500 index. It gives you five trades a month and has an expectancy of 2R. That means that on average you probably can make 10R from that system each month. But what if the system also works on other major stock market indexes with the same results? If you can add 10 more indexes to trade, you may be able to make 100R each month.

3. **Third, add traders.** Each trader can handle only so much work and so many markets effectively. Let's say a good trader can trade $50 million effectively. When the total goes above that level, your experience is that the trader's effectiveness seems to drop off. One way to grow your business is to have more traders. Ten good traders now may be able to handle $500 million effectively.

4. **Fourth, make your traders more effective at what they are doing.** Let's say a trading system generates an average return of 40% each year. You can measure the effectiveness of a trader by the number of mistakes that trader makes. For example, a typical trader may make 20% worth of mistakes each year on a 40% system.

ADD MORE TRADERS

That kind of trader, at 80% effectiveness, would allow you to generate 32% from the system. But what if you could make the trader more effective? What would happen if you gave your traders effective coaching that could reduce their mistakes to 5% each year? That amounts to a 75% increase in effectiveness per trader per system per year. You can expand a trading business immensely through coaching that allows your traders to become more effective.

5. **Fifth, optimize your position sizing for meeting your objectives.** To do that, you must take each of the following steps:

   ● Clearly determine what the objectives are for your business. Many people and many firms do not do this task well.

   ● Determine the R-multiple distribution generated by each of the systems you use.

   ● Simulate different position sizing algorithms to determine which of the thousands of possible algorithms will meet your objectives most effectively.

   ● Apply that algorithm to your systems.

For example, suppose you want to make 200% on your capital allocated to a particular system. You have a system that generates on average 70R each year. If you risk 1% of your allocated capital per trade, you may find that you can make

70% per year from the system. However, if you increase the position sizing risk to 3%, you may find that you can make the 200% you desire. Of course, increasing the position sizing will increase the potential drawdowns. You need to be fully aware of the downside to such changes in position sizing.

All these factors can be multiplicative. For example, suppose you have three traders, each trading two systems in three markets. Each system makes about 60R per year per market, but the traders are only 75% effective in trading them. This means that they make about 15R in mistakes per system per market per year.

Let's look at what is generated for the company. We have three traders times two systems times three markets times 45R. If you multiply these out, you'll find that the company generates 810R each year. Now let's look at the effect of the various changes we could make.

First, what if we added three more traders? We might be able to double the total return to 1,620R.

Second, what if we added three more markets for each system? We might now increase the returns to 3,240R.

What if we added one more system per trader? We might now increase the return to 4,860R.

What would happen if you increased the efficiency of your traders to 90% (which we might have to do for them to handle the extra work)? We'd get an additional 20% more profit and now be at 5,832R.

Finally, what if we made our position sizing more effective to increase our profits another 50%? Well, you get the idea.

No business would be able to do all of the things I've suggested at the same time, but what if you could do a few of them? What would be the impact on your bottom line? If you are considering some of these changes, concentrate on trader efficiency and on more effective position sizing to meet your objectives.

Avoid Making Predictions in the Market

Most people make a big deal out of market prediction. They think they need to be right 70% of the time or more to pass the exam that the market gives them. They also believe that they might get an A if they could be right 95% of the time. The need to predict the market stems from this desire to be right. People believe that they cannot be right unless they can predict what the market is doing.

Among our best clients, I have traders who continually make 50% or more each year with very few losing months. Surely, they must be able to predict the market very well to have that kind of track record. I recently sent out a request for predictions, and here is what I got back from some of the better traders:

> Trader A: I don't predict the market, and I think this is a dangerous exercise.

> Trader B: These are just scenarios; the market is going to do what the market is going to do.

I got these comments from them despite the fact that I was not interested in any of their specific opinions, just the consensus opinion.

How do they make money if they have no opinions about what the market is going to do? There are five critical ingredients involved:

1. They follow the signals generated by the system.

2. They get out when the market proves them wrong.

3. They allow their profits to run as much as possible; that means they have a high positive expectancy system.

4. They have enough opportunity that there is a greater chance of realizing the positive expectancy in any particular month and little chance of having a losing month.

5. They understand position sizing well enough that they will continue to be in the game if they are wrong and make big money when they are right.

Most traders, including most professionals, do not understand these points. As a result, they are very much into prediction. The average Wall Street analyst usually makes a large six-figure income by analyzing companies, yet very few of these individuals, in my opinion, could make money trading the companies they analyze. Nevertheless, people believe that if analysts tell you the fundamentals of the marketplace, they can use that information to make money.

Others have decided that fundamental analysis doesn't work. Instead, they have chosen to draw lines on the computer or in a chart book to analyze the market technically. These people believe that if you draw enough lines and interpret enough patterns, you can predict the market. Again, it doesn't work. Instead, *cutting losses short, riding profits hard, and managing risk so that you continue to survive* is what really makes you money. When you finally understand this at a gut level, you will know one of the key secrets to trading success.

AVOID MARKET PREDICTION

Mistakes and Self-Sabotage

Let's define a mistake as not following your written trading rules. If you develop a working business plan to guide your trading, you'll have numerous rules that you'll need to follow. If you don't develop such rules, everything you do will be a mistake.

There are thousands of possible mistakes you can make. Here are a few common mistakes:

■ Entering on a tip or emotion or something that doesn't correspond to one of your well-thought-out systems

■ Not exiting when you should be stopped out

■ Risking too much money on any particular trade

RISKING TOO MUCH MONEY ON ANY GIVEN TRADE

■ Exiting too soon on emotion

■ Doing anything because of an emotional reaction

■ Not following your daily routine

■ Blaming someone or something for what happens to you rather than accepting personal responsibility

■ Trading multiple systems in the same account

■ Trading so many trades in the same account that you cannot keep track of them

■ Trading a system when the market type has changed and you know that the system now will perform poorly

■ Concentrating on the entry for a system, not the potential reward to risk ratio in the trade

■ Needing to be right and taking a profit too quickly or not taking a loss just to be right

■ Not having a predetermined exit when you enter the trade

■ Not keeping track of the R-multiples and the general performance of your trading system

I've been asking the traders I coach to keep track of their mistakes in terms of R. For example, if you enter the market on emotion and make 2R, that counts as +2R toward that mistake. If you do it again and lose 4R, you now have −2R toward that mistake. If you do that for about a year, you'll have a good idea about how efficient you are as a trader and what your efficiency costs you.

One of my clients was a futures trader who was running a $200 million account. We estimated that over nine months he made 11 mistakes, costing him 46.5R. Thus, he made 1.2 mistakes per month at a cost of 4.23R per mistake. Overall, his profit was probably 50% less than it could have been because of mistakes. Thus, if he made 20%, he probably could have been up 70%. Can you begin to see the impact of such mistakes?

Another client was a long-term position trader who primarily traded ETFs with wide stops. In a year of trading, he made 27 mistakes, costing him 8.2R. Thus, over a year he made 2.25 mistakes per month. However, because he was trading long-term with large stops and no leverage, his mistakes were not as costly. Each mistake was costing him 0.3R. During the year of trading he was up 31R (and about 30%). If he had not made any mistakes, he would have been up 39.2R. Thus, his mistakes cost him 20% of his profits.

What are your mistakes costing you?

How to Prevent Mistakes

I recommend that at the beginning of each day you do a process called mental rehearsal. Ask yourself, "What could go wrong today that might cause me to make a mistake?"

Here is an example. One of my clients in Europe was a superb day trader. He made huge profits daily trading the stock index futures. One day he got a call from a local hospital. His girlfriend had been in a car accident and was seriously injured. He immediately rushed to the hospital to be with her, forgetting about his market positions. He didn't have actual stops in the market. He exited with mental stops because he felt that was generally safer for him. However, on this day, he thought only about his girlfriend.

When he was informed that his girlfriend would be fine, the market was closed. Later, he checked on his positions and discovered that he'd lost about a year's worth of profits that one day.

When I started coaching him, the first thing I had him do was develop a worst-case contingency plan and make sure that every contingency was rehearsed properly. Generally, the better your worst-case contingency plan is, assuming that all your contingency plans are well rehearsed and automatic for you, the less daily mental rehearsal you have to do.

However, my finding is that the market always presents us with events that one would never imagine. As I'm writing this in late 2008, we are having market volatility that is 10 standard deviations bigger than the norm. That has almost a zero probability of occurring when market volatility is normally distributed, but it is occurring. If you are not prepared to trade in this sort of climate, it could be a disaster.

Similarly, who would imagine that the U.S. stock market would close for a while because the World Trader Center was destroyed and the New York financial district was full of rubble? Did you predict that one? Would you be able to predict that a squirrel chewing on wires in your attic could disrupt your trading? It happens, so prepare for it.

Thus, I recommend that everyone do a daily mental rehearsal. Ask yourself, "What could go wrong today to cause me to make a mistake?" Become creative and think of everything. For everything you come up with, rehearse how you'll perform to make sure that it doesn't have a significant impact on your trading.

One day you might meet that big losing trade in the markets that has your number on it. Wouldn't it be a good idea to be prepared for it ahead of time? Increasing your efficiency from 90% (i.e., one mistake every 10 trades) to 98% (i.e., one mistake every 50 trades) could double your return rate or more. This is a second way to think about trader efficiency: mistakes per 100 trades. Earlier I discussed efficiency as the percentage of the total profit realized.

How Not to Repeat Mistakes

There is one more task that you should consider doing on a daily basis. I call this task the daily debriefing. It is designed to ensure that you do not repeat mistakes.

At the end of the trading day, ask yourself a simple question, "Did I make any mistakes?" If the answer is no, pat yourself on the back. If the answer is no and you lost money, pat yourself on the back twice. Good job; you followed your rules.

However, if you did make a mistake, your new task is to make sure that you never repeat it. Ask yourself, "What sorts of conditions were present when I made my mistake? When might they occur again?"

Once you've answered these questions, the task becomes a matter of mental rehearsal, which we discussed earlier. Come up with something you can do to make sure you don't repeat that mistake under those conditions. Once you come up with the solution, rehearse it in your mind a number of times until it becomes second nature to you.

In my opinion, it is essential that you do this task every day. A few minutes each day on this task could end up increasing your returns by 20% to 50% each year.

You Cannot Ignore the Fundamentals

Quite often people make great progress psychologically, but when it comes to some of the fundamental issues that we teach in trading, they ignore them and say, "I don't understand." Most people's response to this statement is to ignore it rather than do whatever is necessary to increase their understanding.

Here is a brief quiz on some key elements that I consider absolute fundamentals for all traders. You must understand these elements if you want to compete as a successful trader. Answer these questions before you read the answers in the next section.

1. You buy a stock for $25. You want a 25% trailing stop. Where is your initial stop?

2. The same stock moves as high as $40 and then goes back down to $37. Where is your stop?

3. You have a $25,000 account and don't want to risk more than 1% of your account on that stock. How much of your account can you risk?

4. In light of your answers to question 1 and 3, how many shares did you buy?

5. You buy another stock for $38, but this time your stop is only 50 cents away. How many shares can you buy to risk only 1%?

6. You think that's too many shares, and so you want to base your stop on the volatility. The average true range over the last 10 days of the stock has been $3. You decide to base your allocation on volatility. How many shares can you buy?

7. Since your stop is still at 50 cents, how much are you risking on this position?

8. What's your total investment amount for the first stock and for the second stock? How is this different from risk?

9. What is the variable that accounts for most of the performance variability you are likely to encounter (assuming that you have your psychology together)?

10. What have I defined self-sabotage to be?

Bonus question: You sell the first stock for $50, or a $25 profit. What is your R-multiple? In other words, your profit is what multiple of your initial risk?

The Answers

HERE ARE THE ANSWERS

1. Your stop should be the current price times 0.75, or $18.75. If you subtract 25% of the price from the current price, you have your stop, and that's equivalent to 75% of the entry price. Give yourself 10 points if you got it right.

2. You have a 25% trailing stop. That means that each time the stock makes a new high (or closing high if you prefer), you take 25% of that as your stop. This is your new stop. Thus, the prior high was $40 and your new stop is 75% of that, or $30. When the price moves down, you do not change your stop. Give yourself another 10 points if you got it right.

3. Your risk is 1% of $25,000, which is $250. Give yourself 10 points if you got it right.

4. Your risk is $6.25. If you divided your risk per share into your total risk allowed ($250), you would end up with 40 shares. Again, give yourself 10 points for a correct answer.

5. Since your risk is only 50 cents, if you divide 50 cents into $250, you end up with 500 shares. Give yourself 10 points if you got it right.

6. Here you divide your 1% risk, or $250, by $3 per share. Your answer is 83.33333333 shares. Round down to the nearest whole share, and the answer is 83. Give yourself 10 points if you got it right.

7. You actually are risking 83 times 50 cents, or $41.50. Give yourself 10 points for that one. Your allocation went down because it was based on volatility. Your stop stayed the same, and so you actually are risking only $41.50.

8. In the first example, you bought 40 shares of a $25 stock. Your total risk was $250, but your total investment was 40 times $25, or $1,000. Notice that you have a 25% stop and that your risk is 25% of your investment. Give yourself 3 points for that one if you got it right. In the second example, you either bought 500 shares based on risk for a $19,000 investment or bought 83 shares based on volatility for a $3,154 investment. Either one is acceptable, and so if you answered one of those correctly, give yourself 3 points. Total investment is the number of shares (e.g., 40) multiplied by the total cost of the share (e.g., $25). In contrast, risk is the number of shares (e.g., 40) multiplied by how much you are willing to let the price drop before you exit (e.g., $6.25). Give yourself 4 points for this answer.

9. Position sizing. Give yourself 10 points if you got it right.

10. Repeating mistakes. Give yourself 10 points if you answered correctly.

Bonus question: You sell the first stock for $50, or a $25 profit. What is your R-multiple? In other words, your profit is what multiple of your initial risk? If you sold the stock at $50, you made a profit of $25. That's four times your initial risk of $6.25, and so you made a 4R profit. Give yourself 10 more points if you got it right. Thus, your total score could be as high as 110.

If you scored 100 or better, your understanding of these fundamentals is excellent. Keep up the good work. If you scored 80 to 99, you need a little work. Figure out where you are weak and do some homework. If you scored 60 to 79, you need a lot of work. Again, figure out where you are weak and make the effort to understand the material.

If you scored 59 or less, it might be because you are new to trading and these principles. If that's the case, you have significant work to do. If you've been studying this material for some time and still got 50 or less, perhaps trading is not for you.

A Personal Invitation from Van K. Tharp

Join the Van Tharp community by visiting my Web site at www.vantharp.com, where you can read my newsletter, *Tharp's Thoughts;* learn what type of trader you are and download a free trading simulation game to practice position sizing. All of this is free.

Here's more information:

Free Trading Simulation Game

We believe that the best way to learn position sizing is to practice using it to meet your objectives. To help you do that, we've developed a 10-level game. The first three levels are free, and you can download them from our Web site, www.vantharp.com. Try it today!

What Type of Trader Are You?

Visit www.tharptradertest.com for more information.

Free *Tharp's Thoughts* Newsletter

Subscribe to *Tharp's Thoughts*, my free e-mail newsletter, and receive tips, articles, market updates, and information on systems development, position sizing, R multiples, and many other trading topics.

The Van Tharp Institute (International Institute of Trading Mastery, Inc.)
102-A Commonwealth Court Cary, NC 27511
Phone: 919-466-0043 or 800-385-IITM (4486)
Fax: 919-466-0408
E-mail: info@iitm.com

Glossary

Algorithm   A rule or set of rules for computing, that is, a procedure for calculating a mathematical function.

Arbitrage   Taking advantage of discrepancies in price or loopholes in the system to make consistent low-risk money. This strategy usually involves the simultaneous purchase and sale of related items.

Asset allocation   The procedure by which many professional traders decide how to allocate their capital. As a result of the lotto bias, many people think of this as a decision about which asset class (such as energy stocks or gold) to select. However, its real power comes when people use it to tell them how much to invest in each asset class. Thus, it is really another term for position sizing.

Average true range (ATR)   The average over the last X days of the true range, which is the largest of the following: (1) today's high minus today's low, (2) today's high minus yesterday's close, (3) today's low minus yesterday's close.

Band trading   A style of trading in which the instrument being traded is thought to move within a range of prices. Thus, when the price gets too high (that is, overbought), you can assume that it will go down. When the price gets too low (that is, oversold), you can assume that it will move up. This concept is discussed in Part 5 of this book.

Bearish   Of the opinion that the market will be going down in the future.

Breakout   A move up from a consolidation or band of sideways movement.

Bullish   Of the opinion that the market will be going up in the future.

Commodities   Physical products that are traded at a futures exchange. Examples are grains, foods, meats, and metals.

Contract   A single unit of a commodity or future. For example, a single unit or contract of corn is 5,000 bushels. A single unit of gold is 100 ounces.

Discretionary trading   Trading that depends on the instincts of the trader, as opposed to a systematic approach. The best discretionary traders are those who develop a systematic approach and then use discretion in their exits and position sizing to improve their performance.

Divergence   A term used to describe two or more indicators that fail to show confirming signals.

Diversification   Investing in independent markets to reduce the overall risk.

Drawdown   A decrease in the value of your account because of losing trades or because of "paper losses" that may result from of a decline in the value of open positions.

Entry   The part of your system that signals how or when you should enter the market.

Equal units model   A position sizing model in which you purchase an equal dollar amount of each position.

Equities   Stocks secured by ownership in the company.

Equity   The value of your account.

Exit   The part of your trading system that tells you how or when to exit the market.

Expectancy   How much you can expect to make on average over many trades. Expectancy is best stated in terms of how much you can make per dollar you risk. Expectancy is the mean R of an R-multiple distribution generated by a trading system.

Filter   An indicator that selects only data that meet specific criteria. Too many filters tend to lead to overoptimization.

Financial freedom   A financial state that occurs, according to Van Tharp, when your passive income (income that comes from your money working for you) is greater than your expenses. For example, if your monthly expenses total $4,000 and your money working for you brings in $4,300 per month, you are financially free.

Floor trader   A person who trades on the floor of a commodities exchange. Locals tend to trade their own accounts, and pit brokers tend to trade for a brokerage company or a large firm.

Forex   Foreign exchange; a huge market in foreign currencies made by large banks worldwide. Today there are also much smaller companies that allow you to trade forex, but they take the side of the bid-ask spread opposite from yours.

Fundamental analysis   Analysis of the market to determine its supply and demand characteristics. In equities markets, fundamental analysis determines the value, the earnings, the management, and the relative data of a particular stock.

Futures   A contract obligating its holder to buy a specified asset at a particular time and price. When commodity exchanges added stock index contracts and currency contracts, the term was developed to be more inclusive of those assets.

Holy Grail system   A mythical trading system that perfectly follows the market and is always right, producing large gains and zero drawdowns. No such system exists, but the real meaning of the Holy Grail is right on track: It suggests that the secret is inside you. In addition, as we've described in this book, you can easily design a Holy Grail system if it is specific to one market type.

Indicator   A summary of data presented in a supposedly meaningful way to help traders and investors make decisions.

Investing   Refers to a buy-and-hold strategy that most people follow. If you are in and out frequently or are willing to go both long and short, you are trading.

Leverage   A term used to describe the relationship between the amount of money one needs to put up to own something and its underlying value. High leverage, which occurs when a small deposit controls a large investment, increases the potential size of profits and losses.

Liquidity   The ease and availability of trading in an underlying stock or futures contract. When the volume of trading is high, there is usually a lot of liquidity.

Long   Owning a tradable item in anticipation of a future price increase. Also see *short*.

Low-risk idea   An idea that has a positive expectancy and is traded at a risk level that allows for the worst possible situation in the short term so that one can realize the long-term expectancy.

Martingale strategy   A position sizing strategy in which the position size increases after you lose money. In the classic martingale strategy you double your bet size after each loss.

Maximum adverse excursion (MAE)   The maximum loss attributable to price movement against the position during the life of a particular trade.

Mechanical trading   A form of trading in which all actions are determined by a computer with no human decision making.

Mental rehearsal   The psychological process of preplanning an event or strategy in one's mind before actually doing it.

Modeling   The process of determining how some form of peak performance (such as top trading) is accomplished and then the passing on of that training to others.

Money management   A term that has been used to describe position sizing but that has so many other connotations that people fail to understand its full meaning or importance. For example, the term also refers to (1) managing other people's money, (2) controlling risk, (3) managing one's personal finances, and (4) achieving maximum gain.

Negative expectancy system   A system in which you will never make money over the long term. For example, all casino games are designed to be negative expectancy games. Negative expectancy systems also include some highly reliable systems (that is, those with a high hit rate) that tend to have occasional large losses.

Neuro-linguistic programming (NLP)   A form of psychological training developed by the systems analyst Richard Bandler and the linguist John Grinder. It forms the foundation for the science of modeling excellence in human behavior. However, what usually is taught in NLP seminars are the techniques that are developed from the modeling process. For example, we have modeled top trading, system development, position sizing, and wealth building at the Van Tharp Institute. What we teach in our workshops is the process of doing those things, not the modeling process itself.

Opportunity   See *trade opportunity*.

Passive income   Income that occurs because your money is working for you.

Peak-to-trough drawdown   A term that is used to describe one's maximum drawdown from the highest equity peak to the lowest equity trough before reaching a new equity high.

Percent risk model   A position sizing model in which position sizing is determined by limiting the risk on a position to a certain percentage of your equity.

Percent volatility model A position sizing model in which position sizing is determined by limiting the amount of volatility (which is usually defined by the average true range) in a position to a certain percentage of your equity.

Position sizing The most important of the six key elements of successful trading. This term refers to the part of your system that really determines whether you'll meet your objectives. This element determines how large a position you will have throughout the course of a trade. In most cases, algorithms that work for determining position size are based on one's current equity.

Positive expectancy A system or game that will make money over the long term if played at a risk level that is sufficiently low. It also means that the mean R value of a distribution of R-multiples is a positive number.

Prediction A guess about the future. Most people want to make money by guessing future outcomes, that is, prediction. Analysts are employed to predict prices. However, great traders make money by cutting losses short and letting profits run, which has nothing to do with prediction.

Price/earnings (P/E) ratio The ratio of the price of a stock to its earnings. For example, if a $20 stock earns $1 per share each year, it has a price/earnings ratio of 20. The average P/E of the S&P 500 over the last 100 years has been about 17.

R-multiple A term used to express trading results in terms of the initial risk. All profits and losses can be expressed as a multiple of the initial risk (R) taken. For example, a 10R multiple is a profit that is 10 times the initial risk. Thus, if your initial risk was $10, a $100 profit would be a 10R-multiple profit. When you do this, any system can then be described by the R-multiple distribution that it generates. That distribution will have a mean (expectancy) and a standard deviation that will characterize it.

R-value A term used to express the initial risk taken in a particular position as defined by one's initial stop loss.

Random Refers to an event determined by chance. In mathematics, a number that cannot be predicted.

Reliability How accurate something is or how often it wins. Thus, 60% reliability means that something wins 60% of the time.

Reward-to-risk ratio The average return on an account (on a yearly basis) divided by the maximum peak-to-trough drawdown. Any reward-to-risk ratio over 3 as determined by this method is excellent. This term also may refer to the size of the average winning trade divided by the size of the average losing trade.

Risk The difference in price between the entry point in a position and the worst-case loss one is willing to take in that position. For example, if you buy a stock at $20 and decide to get out if it drops to $18, your risk is $2 per share. Note that this definition is much different from the typical academic definition of risk as the variability of the market in which you are investing.

Scalping   A term that refers to the actions of floor traders who buy and sell quickly to get the bid and ask prices or to make a quick profit. The bid price is what they will buy for (and what you'll get as a seller), and the ask price is what they'll sell for (and what you'll get as a buyer).

Seasonal trading   Trading based on consistent, predictable changes in price during the year that result from production cycles or demand cycles.

Secular (bull or bear) market   A term that refers to long-term tendencies in the market to increase valuations (bull) or decrease valuations (bear). Secular tendencies can last for several decades, but they say nothing about what the market will do in the next few months or even the next year.

Setup   A term that refers to a part of your trading system in which certain criteria must be present before you look for an entry into the market. People used to describe trading systems by their setups. For example, CAN SLIM is an acronym for the setup criteria devised by William O'Neil.

Short   Not actually owning an item that you are selling. If you were using this strategy, you would sell an item in order to be able to buy it later at a lower price. When you sell an item before you actually have bought it, you are said to be shorting the market.

Sideways market   A market that moves neither up nor down.

Slippage   The difference in price between what you expect to pay when you enter the market and what you actually pay. For example, if you attempted to buy at 15 and end up buying at 15.5, you have a half point of slippage.

Speculating   Investing in markets that are considered very volatile and thus quite risky in the academic sense of the word.

Spreading   The process of trading two related markets to exploit a new relationship. Thus, you might trade Japanese yen in terms of British pounds. In doing so, you are trading the relationship between the two currencies.

Standard deviation   The positive square root of the expected value of the square of the difference between a random variable and its mean. A measure of variability that has been expressed in a normalized form.

Stop (stop loss, stop order)   An order you put with your broker that turns into a market order if the price hits the stop point. It's typically called a stop (or stop loss order) because most traders use it to make sure they sell an open position before it gets away from them. It typically will stop a loss from getting too big. However, since it turns into a market order when the stop price is hit, you are not guaranteed that you'll get that price. It might be much worse. Most electronic brokerage systems will allow you to put a stop order into their computer. The computer then sends it out as a market order when that price is hit. Thus, it does not go into the market, where everyone might see it and look for it.

Support   The price level that a stock historically has had difficulty falling below. It is the area on the chart at which buyers seem to come into the market.

Swing trading   A term that refers to short-term trading designed to capture quick moves in the market.

System   A set of rules for trading. A complete system typically has (1) some setup conditions, (2) an entry signal, (3) a worst-case disaster stop loss to preserve capital, (4) a profit-taking exit, and (5) a position sizing algorithm. However, many commercially available systems do not meet all these criteria. A trading system also may be described by the R-multiple distribution it generates.

Trade distribution   A term that refers to the manner in which winning and losing trades are achieved over time. It will show the winning streaks and the losing streaks.

Trade opportunity   One of the six keys to profitable trading. It refers to how often a system will open a position in the market.

Trading   Opening a position in the market, either long or short, with the expectation of either closing it out at a substantial profit or cutting losses short if the trade does not work out.

Trading cost   The cost of trading, which typically includes brokerage commissions and slippage, plus the market maker's cost.

Trailing stop   A stop loss order that moves with the prevailing trend of the market. It typically is used as a way to exit profitable trades. The stop is moved only when the market goes in your favor. It is never moved in the opposite direction.

Trend following   The systematic process of capturing extreme moves in the market with the idea of staying in the market as long as the market continues its move.

Units per fixed amount of money model   A position sizing model in which you typically buy one unit of everything per so much money in your account. For example, you might buy one unit (that is, 100 shares or one contract) per $25,000.

Validity   A term that indicates how "real" something is. Does it measure what it is supposed to measure? How accurate is it?

Valuation   An exercise in giving some value on the price of a stock or commodity that is based on some model for determining value. See *value trading*.

Value trading   A term that refers to a concept in which positions are opened in the market because they have good value. There are numerous ways to measure value. A good way of thinking about it is that if the assets of a company are worth $20 per share and you can buy the company for $15 per share, you are getting a good value. Different value traders have different ways to define value.

Volatility   A term that refers to the range of prices in a particular time period. A high-volatility market has a large range in daily prices, whereas a low-volatility market has a small range of daily prices. This is one of the most useful concepts in trading. Volatility generally describes the noise in the markets.

Index